Enter The Vortex
as
One Light

A Journey to
Interdimensional Freedom

By

Sizzond Zadore

Light Pulsations
Tasmania, Australia

First published in Australia in 1997 by
Light Pulsations Ionic Healing Pty Ltd.
85 York Street Launceston, Tasmania,
Australia. 7250

Facsimile. + 61- 3 632 81539

Cover © Lola Jesse

Our special thanks to Nadine Jesse for the many hours of toil
which she gave freely in the editing of this
manuscript

ISBN 0 646 31591 9
Printed and Bound in Australia by Northern Wholesale
Stationery, Launceston, Tasmania.

Dedication

"To the Earth"

"Are you deaf to my calls for help? Do so few know and even less care? Will you make the change and move your consciousness and Light back to me? Turn your Ego away from that Illusion and take control of your own Light! My Light is your Light, or will you give your Ego to the Astral Lords? For it will become aligned to the Astral Frequency and be lost to its normal connection on the higher dimension. Move your consciousness into the Vortex of Light and Healing. Move away from all Illusion and send your Light back to me. Become the Vortex and the Astrals will cease to exist in your consciousness. You will be filled with Love and Light, be free from fear, hate and greed. I have only suffered this loss and indignity because you sought power outside yourself and not inwardly as One Light."

"Soul of Earth"

NEXUS MAGAZINE
55 Queens Road
East Grinstead
West Sussex. RH19 1BG
Tel: 01342-322854

Contents

Foreword.

I love this book. I love the spirit in which it is written - a spirit of respect for human life and for the earth, a spirit which affirms the validity of personal choice, honours an individual soul's passage on the earth and offers to facilitate its unfolding both by bringing important information and by encouraging the development of awareness in anyone who seeks to become fully what he or she is. It does this with no strings attached. Thomas Jefferson once said, "A country cannot be both ignorant and free...." The same might be said of a human being.

As we approach the millennium, book shelves creak beneath *channelled* material - information that is said to have been given by some 'higher being' as a gift to people. I tend to listen to such words with the same mixture of curiosity and sceptisim I call up when my latest taxi driver tells me the 'inside story' about what *really* happened in the news which none of the papers printed. And I find, in terms of unbiased accuracy and fair comment, the quality of information gleaned from taxi drivers tends to be about equal to that from channels. Yet there is, in the end, one big difference: A taxi driver never asks that you give up your power of personal choice. He does not try to sell you some political or religious creed without the full acceptance of which you are doomed. Nor does he set himself up as some outside authority whom you are asked to believe without question or surrender your life to.

The same can not be said for much channelled information nor for most of the information that is disseminated by our religious institutions and political systems. Guidance from such sources is, more often than not, designed not to give people back their autonomy - empowering their freedom and leading them to the beauty of their own essential being - but rather to erode human freedom and make us feel that we are not enough as we are, or that we are weak, or wrong, or like poor helpless sheep. It tends to encourage us to ignore the whispers of our own soul and follow instead some outside authority claiming to be a shepherd who offers salvation from the wolves. Meanwhile the wolves gorge their bellies on us - we self-effacing sheep - thus narrowing the freedom we are allowed to buying a pair of Levi 501's or drinking the latest mixture of rum and fruit juice which we see drunk by bikini-clad people on tropical beaches when we turn on the TV.

Not so the transmissions of Zadore. They are clearly designed to facilitate human freedom - the only kind of real freedom there is - namely freedom to become fully what one is in one's essential nature and in the process to nurture both ourselves and the earth of which we are a part. The words in this book inspire, inform and empower. They do not exploit or manipulate.

Zadore refers to those energies which do exploit human life by twisting men, gold, and ideas to their own ends as Astral Lords. I came to know these Astral Lords only too well during the four and a half years that it took me to write my first novel *Ludwig...A Spiritual Thriller*. I was thrown headlong into the unseen world which they inhabit, made to look soberly at how they manipulate our environment, our thinking, our governments, our religions. Then I found myself face to face with choice: Do I follow conventions blindly in the hope of finding safety, security and protection from the dangers I perceived around me? or do I choose another way even if it means - as

King Arthur's knights opted for - entering the forest where it is darkest, never dreaming to follow a path mapped out by someone else. To do so, they believed, would be to dishonour the search for The Grail.

I chose to enter that forest and leapt into the process of transformation and growth which each of us has to go through in our own individual way if we are to manifest on the earth the full beauty of our essential being and to care for our planet. It is a process I am still utterly committed to and the most exciting journey I have ever been on. It is to others, who, like me, are seeking their own path towards freedom and truth that Zadore's words speak most loudly. Zadore's words encourage such a process, They inform, They inspire, They empower. They are words of which anyone committed to true human freedom would be proud.

Pity Thomas Jefferson could not have stuck around to hear them.

Leslie Kenton,
Pembrokeshire, Wales.
United Kingdom.

March, 1997.

Publishers Note

Dear Reader,

If you have read the exciting story of "One Light", by Jon Whistler, you will already have been introduced to the Transmissions of Zadore and will be prepared for a deeper understanding of the Vortex and its important meaning of Light and Healing for this planet.

This second book contains no story but consists solely of Transmissions given by the Being of the Fifth-dimension, Zadore, and Sizzond, which is Zadore's Light-consciousness of the Fourth-dimension. There is no channelling involved in this work, and the reason for this can best be explained by a reading of "One Light". If possible, it would be preferable for you to acquire a copy of "One Light" also and read this first, however it is not absolutely necessary. A short introduction written by Jon Whistler and Rose Medlin will put you in the picture and the Transmissions will explain themselves as you delve into their wonderful revelations.

Many people have written to us and, through us, to Jon and Rose since the publishing of "One Light expressing their appreciation of the Transmissions and the joy and liberation they have experienced since reading that book. However "One Light" was merely the beginning, and "Enter the Vortex as One Light" continues the joy, deepening and widening the under-standings first presented in "One Light", drawing the reader into an unfolding vision of the Self, the Earth and the Universes that is truly magnificent and freeing.

The Publisher.
Postscript.

The Transmissions are presented as given, with personal references using the pronouns I, you and me. These refer to Jon and
Rose, however the reader has been included in the editing of
this book. The Transmissions are meant for everyone, everywhere, and you should consider that they are directed personally at you. These are your Transmissions; this is your Vortex.
You have your own Light Essence and as you enter the Vortex
you will receive your own direct inspiration.

Introduction

The month of June 1994 brought with it the first appearance of the Transmissions of Zadore on the planet Earth and began for three people an adventure in consciousness which since has not lessened in intensity with the passing of time. Rather, the two of us who remain in this Third-dimension have seen the adventure magnify and multiply as more and more individuals - those who have read "One Light" and taken the message to heart - become involved in the re-awakening of their own consciousness to the rememberance of Self and Its purpose here on Earth.

One of the most daunting revelations of "One Light" was that Mankind stands at the crossroads of a fateful event that in some respects is not the result of its own transgressions. The only transgression Mankind has committed is of denying its true purpose for being on this planet and forgetting what that purpose is - to direct the Light and Consciousness of the Stars of this Galaxy to the Earth. In "One Light" we learned that the Earth is a living Being, one that over periods of time has been badly assaulted, first by the Astral Lords, and then, through their coercion, by human beings.

Now, once more, the Astral Lords, through their subservient Entities who hold high positions in government, the military and monetary organizations of the world, are set to either destroy or cripple the Earth in their attempt to break free from the radiation belts which act as their prison in the Astral atmosphere surrounding the Earth. *"Set us free - or we will destroy the planet!"* is their ultimatum.

As Zadore's message unfolded in "One Light" we saw that there were two options open to the Galactic Lords for dealing with this ultimatum. One is that they move the Earth from its current orbit, resulting in climatic changes, earthquakes and other catastrophic events, and consequently destroying most of the planetary life. The second is that Zadore should present an alternative way for the humans, one which will guide them back to their true purpose and save the planet from destruction.

Thus Zadore created a Vortex of Light and Healing which is already moving the consciousness of many on the Earth. This Vortex will allow those who seek to save the planet to re-awaken their Light Body and move through the Vortex to self-luminosity. It will not take many such Light Beings to destroy the power of the Astrals and lead the rest of Mankind through the Vortex to freedom. Then all will move with the Earth as it ascends into the frequencies of the Fourth-dimension.

What we have learned from "One Light" is that should the Galactic Lords shift the axis of the planet once more, consciousness will be moved backwards into a prior state of existence whereby it will take many thousands of years to return to the current stage of awareness. Having seen how the Astral Lords have worked in the past, Zadore, at the command of the Galactic Lords, has moved the energies of the Vortex from the Fifth-dimension, through the Solar Gate of the Sun, to the Earth, in order to activate the neural patterns within us for our return to our Light.

Each one of us must be ready to enter into the New Paradigm on Earth, which means all consciousness free from old habits, old rituals, and the old control systems that belong to the matrix of the old paradigm. As an example, in the old and decaying paradigm, sickness, as a condition, is used to enslave the consciousness of Mankind in a perpetual state of negativity. Through its widespread acceptance, sickness becomes an integral part of the Earth experience, enslaving consciousness deeper in the Illusion.

It is time to embrace the New Paradigm, the paradigm which places Man in the true perspective, which recognizes that you are already a divine being, and that all that is necessary is for you to recognize the Illusion that keeps you separate from your Light Essence - broken into segments of consciousness scattered across the dimensions of your Being.

*

Following the publication of this book, at a later date, there will be presented a boxed set of cards which will provide you with the tools to make the journey back to your Light and give that Light to the Earth. The boxed set of cards will be called "The Oracle to Freedom". The oracle cards and an accompanying booklet will assist you to focus daily on the various aspects of the Vortex which will alter the frequencies of your consciousness in its ascent. Your life must be filled with purpose and desire for you to truly move "home", and by "home" we mean your real home and not the fairy-tale heaven of the Astral prison.

Also in the boxed set you will receive a copy of the Vortex painting - "The Way Through the Vortex".

It is suggested that each day you set aside some time in order to attune your Ego to the Vortex by focusing your consciousness to the painting. In this way you will be able to project your consciousness deeper into the Vortex and your own Being. A full sized, laminated copy of the original painting will be available separately from Light Pulsations.

The Vortex of Zadore is actually grounded in a natural crystalline rock, pyramidal structure located in the Pacific Ocean. The energies of the Fifth-dimension are grounded through the Vortex and are continually being intensified by the crystalline structures within the core of the Earth. The Earth is y radiating these energy frequencies to all life on its surface. These energies are silently causing subtle changes to the DNA. Healing is already at hand in every facet of organic life on the planet and life forms are now experiencing these frequencies. This is causing an awakening to the higher consciousness of the New Paradigm, which will introduce an era of enlightenment, instead of destruction.

Much has been predicted in the past and at the present time, of the coming of a major change in the human consciousness and in the worldly environment. This change is often pictured as being a catastrophic one in which destruction plays a large part, such as Armageddon. However, prediction has become such a popular business that one should seriously question it and, in particular, question the reason for it.

Calendars of events are neither fundamental nor certain nor indisputable, even when carved in stone. They are only the manufacture of Man, as is the notion of Time. Time does not exist in the Cosmos, and Man's attempts to link great events or catastrophes to invented calendars which, in fact, bear no relationship to the great cycles of the Universe, are ultimately futile.

The predictions that arise from these attempts are also misleading, for they lead people to expect and focus on this or that future, and largely to live in fear because of what they expect. This suits the plans of the Astrals admirably - prediction is a part of the Illusion that they perpetuate - for they know that when people focus intently on their fears, and turn them into expectations, they bring them about in their lives.

Before you now is a decision. Are you ready to move through this Vortex into enlightenment? Are you prepared to understand this book and participate in moving your consciousness away from illusion and destruction? Once you begin to awaken your inner light, your consciousness will be changed forever.

All true healing begins with the individual. You must constantly move your energy away from the Illusion and back to your true Light. There is no other way for you at this time. Your movement will erode the power of the Astrals and their human entities. You will move through a progressive act of self healing, a healing on all dimensions of your consciousness. Once you are truly healed you will heal the Earth, for that was the original purpose that you forgot.

Jon Whistler and Rose Medlin.

Transmission
One

The Opening

Greetings:

It is now time for you to begin your journey to freedom and light, for you must learn how to enter the Vortex of Light and Healing. Most individuals have different concepts of what exactly constitutes a vortex. Generally it is considered to being a whirling mass of water or air as is seen with a whirlpool or whirlwind. This understanding relates to a Third-dimensional manifestation of energies. The Vortex of Light and Healing consists of energies of varying frequencies moving in a spiral formation. These spiralling frequencies have opposite polarities which, due to their attraction and repulsion attributes, create an energy pattern which is the Vortex.

What this means is that the opposite forces in themselves have no power, for all power is created in the space between them. The one common factor shared by all vortices is that they have the power to draw everything into their central core. This central core is the focus point of the vortex, for it is here where everything begins and ends. It is here at this central point that you exist in the Light of Brahman.

The polarities of the Vortex consist of two energies, that

of Light and Healing. Light is the positive outflow of pure radiant energy from Brahman, and due to its different frequency, Healing becomes a "negative" or slower frequency in its polarity. Light is an ever expanding energy which underlies the frequencies found in all Dimensions. Healing, as distinct from health, is not a condition, but a frequency which is the recognition that something is not whole, that there is a need to move the required elements toward the perfect Light. You can observe Healing through the changing of imperfection to wholeness. It is the combination or these two frequencies which produces the power of the Vortex.

Before you can enter the Vortex of Light and Healing, you need to develop some concept of how the Vortex manifests. As your consciousness is grounded in the Third-dimension, you as most individuals, may use the process of visualization to create a reality or picture to represent what you are attempting to realize. If you persist in using this process you will not be able to attune with the Vortex, for the energies of the Higher Dimensions differ from those of the Third-dimension and their manifestation as matter.

As you become aware of your life patterns relative to your behavior, attitudes and karmic involvement, you will be able to move your consciousness deeper into the changing whorls of the Vortex, and move into the power of its core. Initially you will accomplish this by altering the habitual behavior patterns of your Ego, for unless you start here, your Ego, through its participation in the Astral Illusion, will prevent your entry.

Before looking any further at this entry point I will draw your attention, Jon, to the experience that you underwent with Razparil at the time of your "accident". It was difficult for you to realize that although you felt whole and one, you could see your physical body trapped in the car. Your first thought was that you were dead. However you felt no different to how you felt when you left the site office. So what you now understand is that you had no loss of consciousness at that time. So too when your body dies you still feel that you are YOU, for that is all that you generally feel yourself to be. This is a part of the trap of the Illusion of the Astral Lords, for you can be led into the Fourth-dimensional atmosphere of the Astrals and continue experiencing the Illusion that they have created in your consciousness for thousands of years.

On the death of the Earth body you first re-live your life, behavior and experiences, and make a quasi-atonement based on a feeling of sorrow at an emotional level (I say this, for true atonement for mistakes and misdeeds can only be completely cleared on the Dimension where they originally occurred). At that instant the vapours of the Fourth-dimension open to your consciousness and your "soul" moves to that level of frequency where you expected your "heaven" to be. This is often just a continuation of the Illusion on the Third-dimension. Some thousands of years ago the mass consciousness of mankind expected to see beautiful beings such as angels, and to live with these light beings in the presence of God for all eternity. Many people still remain in this state of expectation until they fall "asleep" and return to the Third-dimension. Currently the Astral Lords have created a "heaven" which mirrors some of the recent changes in Twentieth century thought, building illusionary crystal cities inhabited by "Light Beings" who are "teachers" or "instructors". Everything on both dimensions is done to maintain the Illusion. However eventually the "soul" falls asleep to any other experience of the Astral Illusion, or even to its higher light, and awakens again in another body, ready to repeat the same deception.

The Opening

There are some individuals who have moved away from a commitment to Astral concepts, to some degree, during their Life-experience in the Third-dimension. Since they are no longer wholly blinded by the Illusion, at the death of their Earth-body they do not become trapped in the Illusion on the Fourth-dimension. How far they move from the Astral atmosphere depends upon what degree of diassociation from the Illusion their Ego has experienced. These individuals are able then to move into the levels of the Fourth-dimension which emit more light.

When you were confronted with a being who was aware of your awakening and knew that you were still fragmented from your Fourth-dimensional consciousness, this being, Razparil, felt confident that he would be able to hold you in his astral grip of fear. However you awakened your Fourth-dimensional Light, Sizzond, which had been ignored for many thousands of years, and this became one with your Ego. Once this occurs to everyone, they will never again move into the Astral atmosphere of the Illusion, but will remain as one with their higher consciousness. Even if it is necessary to move back to an Earth body they will be unaffected by the Astral Illusion.

Therefore your entry point into the Vortex begins at the level of your Ego, and it is your understanding of the Illusion that is of prime importance for your freedom.

As I have previously stated, you cannot visualize the Vortex, for it is too vast in its essence for the Intellectual polarity of your Ego to comprehend. Nevertheless, your Ego will try, and that will set up a hindrance that you quickly need to break down. In its attempts, the intellectual polarity of the Ego will try to make innovative changes to its understanding of the Vortex in order to fit the concept into the Illusion. You see, having created the Illusion, the Astrals do not have to continue maintaining it, for they have willing workers in your intellectual Ego response which will continually twist anything outside the Illusion to fit into it. When this occurs you once again fall back into the Illusion.

Also, the intellectual polarity of the Ego, which is often described as left brain behavior in human beings, will first convince others that it has the knowledge and keys for entry into the Vortex. This Ego feels that it is a dominant force in the emerging group of Egos and considers that, as a leader, it is able to choose who is worthy enough to move into the Vortex, and under what conditions. This is a common ploy of the Astrals and was used by them as they moved independent attunement with the Christ principle away from being a personal experience into of having to belong to a Faith headed by Popes, and, later, Elders etc. who control and formulate all the rules needed to become one with the Christ. That is how the mind of the Ego functions, and to enter into the Vortex you must discount that element. It is extremely important for you to cast aside all aspects of the intellect in your movement into the Vortex. Unless you do this you will not move into its energy transformations.

Because of the changing frequencies occurring to the consciousness of the Planet, those "leaders" of New Age Thought are continually telling others that they must seek to uncover or find their Soul. In all instances people do not know just what this soul is that they need to find, in fact they are confusing their soul with their Light Being, for they are still using the Astral controlled church model of the soul. This leads the true seekers down the wrong path, and in their confusion they become willing to accept anything which fits their concept of soul, even when that concept is Astrally manipulated.

The soul of Man is the Ego. To place it more clearly,

what Man terms "soul" is the Ego. Most people will not be able to define just what the Ego is, for they understand it to be that part of themselves which just wants everything, and often their Ego is placed in the status of being the devil. You will remember from the Transmissions that there was reference to the Ego as being a Lens which was created for translating information received through the five senses of the body for the dimensional bodies on the Fourth and higher dimensions. Also it is supposed to move information from the higher dimensions back to the Earth through the body.

There is a separation in the Third-dimensional consciousness by which a distinction is made between the Mind and Soul in man. What you must first understand is that the Mind and Soul are one unit, and that unit is the Ego. Mind has always been seen as a separate, undefinable thing which is distinct from the brain, but requires the brain for expression. The Soul in Man has been referred to as that feeling of inner joy and love that is expressed through the body. Both these descriptions are basically correct in their expression or manifestation, however they are a dual expression of the Ego.

The Mind of Man can be understood as that intellectual polarity of the Ego, and the Soul of Man as the loving, feeling polarity of the Ego. In the body both these aspects of the Ego are reflected by the brain. It is a common understanding of your scientific circles that the brain has a left and right hemisphere, reflecting intellectual expression on one side and creative expression on the other.

The Ego is a permanent part of the One Light which allows the function of your being on all dimensions. The joyful, loving nature of the Ego in most individuals is constantly suppressed by the intellectual mind polarity. The feeling polarity has lived in denial of its full expression for eons of time.

Enter The Vortex as One Light

Let us consider just what this means. The feeling polarity of the Ego is currently being hailed as the Goddess in everyone, whether in a male or female body. What must be understood is that this Goddess is suppressed in both men and women, although some of the latter attempt to dispute this. Men always consider that this Goddess belongs solely to the female sex. Thus, by claiming intellectual mind control as male property and disclaiming emotion they believe that this puts the male into the God classification, and this pleases them for they consider that to be the dominant role. However it is the mind function of the Ego which initially moved to the Astral "temptation" many thousands of years ago.

It is time to destroy the myth that led the human Ego away from its original purpose, and that is the myth of the Garden of Eden. This was the first recording of the Ego's movement away from self consciousness on all dimensions into a one dimensional consciousness. The translation or the original writing was altered in order that the Astral Lords could maintain the Illusion. It was the intellectual polarity of the Ego which took the "forbidden fruit" - the grab at power and dominance over the Earth and all on it. The intellectual polarity encouraged the feeling polarity to move with it into a darkness and hell of the Astral Lords. Since then the intellectual polarity of the Ego, be the body male or female, has blamed the feeling polarity of the Ego for not stopping it from following the Astral way. Since then, in the mass consciousness of Mankind, the result of this event has been constantly used to create a bondage over the feeling polarity. The bondage has been extended right down to that of the physical body. Constantly it has been used to control and subdue the feminine consciousness of the race. By doing this, the feeling polarity is held captive, preventing too much expression of love and joy on the Third-dimension and any contact with the higher light essences of the One Light.

To enter the Vortex you must begin to allow the feeling polarity to express itself without interference from the intellectual polarity. There must be no dominance by either polarity, for they are actually one, and it is by their separation that they create the tensions within themselves.

You must begin to quieten the constant babbling of the intellectual mind aspect of the Ego. Often individuals attempt to tell it to stop only to find seconds later that it continues its non stop verbalizing. It is important for you to remember that it encouraged the feeling polarity to join with it in Earth domination - so it does nothing alone.

When you wish to become quiet, and you listen to the constant chatter passing through your consciousness, ask, "What am I feeling about this intellectual rambling?" Try and move into a feeling frequency. Challenge it with how you feel about what is being said. You will find that there will always be a feeling attached to the thoughts which the intellectual Ego polarity is expressing. When you begin to capture the feelings attached you will begin to take control. Not all of the feelings you find will be good or positive. However realizing this is part of your cleansing, for you will be able to eradicate much of the negativity that unconsciously dominates your consciousness, and will begin to lessen your karma. For as you move out negative feelings that give power to negative thoughts, you begin to open yourself to your true soul on the next dimension.

At a certain point in the cleansing you will move both the intellectual and feeling aspects of the Ego into a state of surrender. Such a surrender is an opening to the Vortex, for the Vortex will now exist within you, and will flow between the two polarities of the Ego. You will then begin to desire above all else to be one with all that is you. When you first received the transmissions you were constantly directing your thoughts to me on the Fifth-dimension. However, once you awakened Sizzond on the Fourth-dimension, then I was no longer distant from you but existed within you as One Light.

For all who will read this message the same path must be followed, for to know the Vortex you must become it. You will surrender many of those aims and needs that the Ego has placed as being important in your life. Once you see that which you desire above all else, then all other things become diminished in the greater Light of your true being. Remember, the Christ said that if you desire Him alone, then all other things will be added. So begin to see those things which you feel are important in your life and compare them to the Light of your desire. Then follow the strongest Light desire.

Once you grasp and feel what this means you will understand how illness is inflicted on Mankind, and you will see and experience the illness of your own behavior. Society is constantly at war with itself because it lives in denial of its feeling polarity. The thing which precipitates this denial is fed by what we call group activity, for whenever human beings group together, they allow Astral dominance. A group can be in any form. It can be a country, a race, a religious group, a professional organization etc. In fact, whenever two or more people group together in an organized activity, it is very easy to observe the "politicking" and "power behaviours" that the group purpose very quickly degenerates into. This is an example of the dominance of the Ego and is subsequent to Astral control.

Even in the quest for achieving "equality" and some well deserved justice for the female aspects of Mankind, the Feminist movement has been led into the trap of using the assertive intellectual polarity of the Ego to try and achieve their "aims". This only plays into the hands of the Astral Illusion

The Opening

because they are still denying the positive aspect of the feeling polarity, thereby reinforcing the false belief that "intellect is better and more powerful" and "this is the way the world should be."

There is only one answer to this situation and that is to move the intellect and feeling into perfect harmony and allow the reality of your being to unfold. Then and only then will you begin healing, and not only your healing but also healing for the Earth.

When your intellectual polarity desired the Astral Illusion you effectively cut off all contact with your Light Essence. Your Ego became the Ego of the Astral Lords, and when your body dies your Ego lands in their atmosphere on the Fourth-dimension.

This does naught for the Ascension of the Earth, however it is NOW time for you to move into the Vortex, and much that I will send you in these Transmissions will help you on your journey to Freedom and Light. You may be surprised to learn that you are already a beautiful being of Light, you do not have to craft anything. Only *want it - seek it - and love it -* for in so doing you will commence your healing and forward movement into Light.

Once you blend your Ego into one it will become your friend. Do not deny it, do not blame it, but forgive it. Watch every day just how it leads your thoughts and actions on the well trodden path of the Illusion. This will be your first step back - this will be your opening.

Zadore.

Transmission Two

The Grounding

At the command of the Galactic Lords I have created the Vortex of Light and Healing which is beamed from the Fifth-dimension through the frequencies of the Fourth-dimension to the Earth. Although the energies of the Vortex are focused on the Earth, its fields affect consciousness on other Third-dimensional planets within the Galaxy. It was necessary that it be grounded on the Earth in order that you may experience the power of One Light in your consciousness, and through this experience you will increase the Light of the Earth as it is fast approaching an upliftment in its consciousness. After being grounded in a natural pyramidal structure in the Pacific Ocean, the energies penetrated the surface crust of the Earth then began moving into the inner crystalline core of the planet. Here they intensify the energy field of the earth and radiate out these energies to be received by the cellular organisms on the surface.

The Earth is criss-crossed with energy corridors which unite at specific points called "nodal points". These nodal points resonate harmonically with similar nodal points throughout the Galaxy and Brahman. The body to which you currently project your consciousness has corresponding nodal points which your culture calls acupuncture points. These and their meridians are tuned harmonically with the Earth grids. From this network all information from your higher dimensional selves moves into the Earth consciousness.

At these Earth nodal points the energies of the Vortex become concentrated and begin to resonate with the physical body. Thus the Earth and the physical Earth-body are already attuned with the Vortex. It is now time for you to attune your Ego with the Vortex and move the energy from the higher dimensions directly to the consciousness of the Earth.

The Astral Lords have been aware that certain energies can be concentrated at these nodal points of the Earth, as well as at other corresponding points throughout the Galaxy with which they resonate. Initially, the Astrals had stone structures built over these points to attract energies from other parts of the Galaxy. Most of their interest in these energy points was to help them in their continued attempts of escape from their prison on the Fourth-dimension. Currently these structures exist for the passage of energies to pass from the Earth to the Astrals on the Fourth-dimension and can be re-activated by the Astrals if and when the need arises.

Also these stone structures act as "gates" or "doorways" which enable the Astral Lords to move their energies into the Third-dimension. More succinctly, they are vortices which interact with the Fourth-dimension. However, by having the stone structures built on nodal points, they can use them to block specific energies or information reaching the consciousness of the Earth, keeping in mind just how these nodal points act as Resonators throughout the Universe. The frequency pattern of the Astral Lords is such that they cannot project their consciousness directly into an Earth-body. The only way they can manipulate Human Egos is through dreams, when the Ego is in consciousness on the Fourth-dimension. Some Egos sought the path of power and control more than others, and have aligned their consciousness with these Astral Lords.

They are now referred to as Astral Entities. These Entities hold positions of power in a worldly sense in order that they can work for the Astral Lords. The Entities feel that if they can assist these beings to escape into the Galaxy then they too will move with them into higher realms of power and will be able to enslave those whom they subdue. These Entities are currently exploding nuclear devices at specific nodal points on the Earth, and this is intended to do two things. Firstly it will weaken the integrity of the Earth's energy structure, producing earthquakes and volcanic eruptions as well as the potential movement of the axis of the planet. Secondly it is causing instability and energy shifts to other planets throughout the Galaxy through the compatible nodal points which resonate with the Earth points. These energy shifts are then creating stress on other planets in the Galaxy and are undermining the Light web of the Galaxy and Third-dimensional Universe.

The energies of the Vortex, having been grounded on the Earth, will have a stabilising effect on such disruption. However, the Earth cannot fight back unless it receives the higher energies from you. You are the counter-balance against the perverse purposes of the Astral Entities. The Vortex is for you, for your consciousness to become free within Brahman, for that is where you are, except for the Ego's attempts to bind you to the Earth body where it can maintain control over all your thoughts and actions.

Entry into the Vortex is conditional on your removing

the karma, or baggage, that you have collected over many lives, and your moving the healing Light to the planet. The Vortex comes at a time which is crucial for the Earth and the Galaxy itself, for all is part of the unfoldment of Brahman.

The Vortex is a confluence of energies from the Galactic core and other stars, especially Sirius, the Dog Star. It must be seen that all the Stars within the Galaxy, of which your Sun is but one, should be likened to a lens or magnifying glass. They focus differing light frequencies to the planet for its life force. The Sun and other stars are bodies of high frequencies and are composed of light energies that may be best described as Third-dimensional etheric energies. These etheric frequencies are Third-dimensional energies which are of opposite polarity to the denser planetary structures. However they are gates or openings to the higher levels of frequency of the Fourth and Fifth-dimensional Universes and they are called "Star Gates".

As you learned from the transmissions, the human body is basically an antennae which receives impulses from the Galaxy to the Earth and acts as a transmitter of energies from the Earth back to the Galaxy. Much of the incoming information is being blocked by the interference of the Astral Entities. Inner information is being constantly disrupted by the Ego. All this is causing sickness to the Earth as it struggles to survive and grow.

It is well known that the constant destruction of the forests is causing major problems to the soil as well as to the oxygen levels in the atmosphere. However there is a much deeper and insidious side to this. The constant raping of the forests is reducing the amount of information that can be received as the antennae are destroyed. The trees move energy through their roots into the mineral elements of the soils. There is an energy field that moves through the surface of the Earth from the South to North Pole. The energies of this field interact with those extended into the ground by the roots of the trees, and are transmitted through the mineral elements to the crystal core of the planet. This could be seen as being the "food" of the planet.

The rape of the Earth has been instigated by the Astral Lords with the assistance of their cohorts who continually gain financially from the process. These lackeys work well with their masters in their overall plan of escape. Now you begin to appreciate the need to move your Ego away from the Illusion toward the expression of your inner light and use the Vortex to propel you quickly to your destination. You need YOU, the Earth needs YOU, for the Earth depends on YOUR healing.

It is necessary that I constantly expose the Illusion of the life that you currently lead, for you still consider it to be the reality of your existence. This is a major hurdle here for you to overcome. I see that each of you equate what I am teaching with something similar to what you have heard before, but in a different manner. You may see similarities to information taught in religious doctrines, secret societies, or new age revelations. When you feel this way you are once more being trapped by your Ego, for it is important to realize that all groups are caught in the Illusion of the Astrals. I have warned before that no group activity in the Earth will produce freedom for you, as all group effort is designed to maintain false structures and Gods. They are all dominated by Astral intent and will only lead you back to another body and another life dominated by the Illusion.

The Vortex and One Light is not supported by any centres or group membership. It has no earthly body as such and is dependent upon self motivation only. It is a movement of the self to Self. If in the future there develop any groups who allege to be connected with One Light or

The Grounding

the Vortex of Light and Healing, know that they are of Astral intent and are working for the destruction of Light.

Your consciousness, and in particular your Ego, has continually been vampired by the Astrals who use it to gain energy to complete their plans.

These Transmissions are designed to open your consciousness and allow it to break free from the bondage of which you are unaware, so that you may express the Light which is many times greater than anything the Astrals possess, and then move the Earth to its freedom.

Many of the powerful nations on this planet are basically under the control of the Astral Lords and their Entities. As I have said before, the Astral intent is to weaken the Earth's energy structure by using Earth technology to attack the major nodal points on the Earth.

Grounded at these nodal points are the major chakra vortices of the Earth which are part of the Earth's Etheric Web. The Etheric Web is essential in the formation of the Light Body of the Earth, and it extends as far as the innermost radiation belt surrounding the Earth. Because the Etheric energies are of a similar frequency to nuclear energy, the Astral Lords assume that by disrupting and weakening the Etheric Web with nuclear explosions to the nodal points, they can move from a Fourth-dimensional prison through the nodes out into the Galaxy at large. They see this as one way for them to clear the radiation belts.

The enduring cold war was supported by the Astrals in the hope that if the two major nations of that time were to wage war at a nuclear level then this would be to their advantage. The Cold War ended due to the Harmonic Convergence in the last decade, and the walls symbolically fell down. Now the Astrals seize on any conflagration to fan the flames of fear and discon-

Enter the Vortex as One Light

tent and promote the spread of nuclear technology.

For many millennia now they have in many ways, planted into the human consciousness the seed of an idea of impending holocaust. This seed has now spread its roots throughout the religious groups, community groups and even the so-called new age groups. All now are awaiting the inevitable breaking of the seventh seal. To each group there will be a special outcome. To the Roman Catholics it will be the last day, the day of judgement where all the bodies come back from the grave; to others it means the second coming of Jesus who will destroy all the unworthy and restore the Garden of Eden on Earth; to the New Age followers, it will be a shift in consciousness, or a transection between two Universes occurring at the point where the Earth stands in the Universe; to others it will be the annihilation of the Earth, and so on.

To the Astrals it will be their time to move out of their prison. Why have they planted this seed of change and destruction? They understand the consciousness in Man more deeply than Man presently does. They know that by continually making this event a reality in the mind of Man, Man will draw the necessary energies together which will complete their continued visualization, thus making it a reality. There is no Divine prophesying here, rather there is a controlled destiny. For by impregnating the consciousness with expectation and continually drawing Mankind into war with itself, the Astral Lords sow the seeds of misery and a definite end to it all - the needed holocaust.

How sad it seems to you to feel that you are trapped in a situation such as this. That sadness is the guilt which your Ego is imposing on you. In the past, you have run with the Astrals and their Illusion, and it has become part of your baggage or karma. The mass of humanity has surrendered to the holocaust

32

The Grounding

of the Astrals instead of surrendering to the One Light. They have surrendered to the Illusion. Have you?

Enter the Vortex and surrender to your Light, and give it to the Earth and all others on the planet in the Illusion. For by giving your light to your sisters and brothers, you are giving yourself to Brahman, and becoming one in creation. Remove the roots and seeds of the impending doom from your consciousness and the consciousness of others, for it must be seen expressedly as only an illusion too, and can be destroyed like any other negative thought form impinging on your consciousness. Fear no more and begin to express joy and love, for the expanding Light consciousness will provide all knowledge for healing, especially that of rendering nuclear wastes harmless, never to be seen again on this planet.

The Earth will continue its Ascension, refining its frequency as it moves to a beautiful Etheric being and later to a Fourth-dimensional Light Being expanding its light as a Star in the Galaxy and becoming a part of the higher consciousness of the Universe.

To achieve this enlightenment there will be continual shifts of energy which will alter the structural composition of its body. Already the Earth's rotation is slowing down, and when it reaches a point of inertia, the radiation belts will be drawn back closer to the surface, altering the polarity of many of the ionic particles that maintain the electromagnetic environment. Once the planet begins to rotate in the opposite direction a new Earth will evolve. The energies of the radiation belts are of the same frequency as the mass of the Sun. As they move closer to the denser frequencies of the Earth they will react, forming patterns that will create altered densities on the Earth's surface. The frequencies of the charged particles will be devoid of the current polarity and will be beginning to reflect energy frequencies similar to those of the Sun. In many millions of years hence the Earth will become a Star System in its own right, producing its own lower dimension planets.

Where will this leave the Astrals? They too are consciousness within Brahman and as such they have the choice of the path they wish to follow. No doubt they can choose to move their Light back to the unconditional love and non-judgmental Brahman, or they can continue their downward progression into deeper density.

As you begin your movement into the Vortex you will pass beyond the radiation belts and back through the Sun, for it is you who are now at the forefront of the grand awakening for the Earth. You would not have been attracted to the Transmissions had you not been ready.

*

To achieve true healing you must unite both polarities of your Ego. Thought and emotion at times appear inseparable because you are not aware which one occurs first. Often a negative emotion can override the mind and there is no control over the subsequent actions. Likewise the mind may block out positive feelings and not express love or compassion. The Ego needs to move its consciousness back to the inner Light of the higher dimensional consciousness. Because it feels that it will lose control over the Third-dimension and its Illusion, it moves against the incoming Light. These attempts at suppression against its Light create great tensions within the whole fabric of the Ego and the body to which it is attached. It is these tensions which cause disharmony, sickness and destruction to the body.

The present level of consciousness on the Earth views

The Grounding

healing solely in terms of the body. People feel that they experience all pain, all energy loss and all degeneration of the tissues that maintain the form and structure of the body as the sole cause and nature of illness.

You do not actually feel the pain when the physical body becomes damaged. The body suffers a trauma to its nervous system which is then passed through to its higher chakras of the Etheric body to create an awareness of the event to the Ego. The Ego is now so involved with its Earth-body that it feels that it is the body. When a major trauma occurs the Ego goes into fear of its possible loss of consciousness, and translates the body trauma into pain. This pain is the Ego's focus on the body part which is injured. Illness and accident patterns create destructive changes to the morphogenetic fields which are the formative patterns that give the body its form. As the morphogenetic field of the body is an Earth field, the Earth can recreate the form or discard it if it is not functionally useful, and make another one. This is not acceptable to the Ego for it cannot easily access that new form, as it "has to get back in the queue". Being aware of this, the Ego of Mankind, in its vanity, continually strives to patch up the degenerating form, spending billions of work energies attempting to devise ways and means of prolonging the cycle of the body. Does anyone ever question why? When people say "I want to live forever", they are saying that they want their Ego and its body to live forever. And in so saying, they strive conversely to suppress the truth, that their being does in fact live forever.

Pain is experienced at the level of the Ego and this should be so, for all illness is the suppression by the Ego of the Light of Brahman. The Ego exists on the Etheric level and lower Fourth-dimension. It is the intermediary focus lens of the light flowing from the higher dimensions.

Enter the Vortex as One Light

All healing must be centred toward the Ego and to accomplish this you will need to turn your gaze toward your Ego and begin to understand it. It is essential that the human body is placed in correct perspective relative to who and what you are. Once you achieve this through positive feeling rather than intellectualizing about it, you will be able to move your energy away from the Illusion.

Transmission Three

The Ego

Currently you believe that all your consciousness revolves around the bodily experiences received through the five senses which act as doorways allowing you to process all information received. You are told continually that you have free will, that is, the ability to determine your destiny. How can one imagine that one is free when one lives in an illusion? You do not have free will in your present state of existence, you only have a choice to decide between the parameters contained in the Illusion, for the Illusion contains the morals and laws based on the definitive society or the country in which you live. Your freedom of choice or will applies to how you wish to behave and be seen by others who live with you in your Illusion. He or she who may be seen as a good citizen in one country may be considered a criminal in another one.

There are many teachers in the world attempting to induce individuals to practice the art of self empowerment. In order to evaluate the worth of any system it is necessary for you to determine just what "self" it is that is being empowered. Often you will discover that some of these systems are directing their energies toward the attainment of specific goals that match the success patterns which are built into the Illusion. It would be correct to rename such systems as "Ego empowerment". For empowerment is gauged to lead you to experience wealth, success and power over others in society, and elevate you to a position of respect and acceptance within the Illusion. This will in no way lead you to your true self, rather the opposite occurs. You have no need to empower your self for it already is powerful and perfect. I am creating an awareness within your consciousness about entering into systems and organizations that will weaken your energies, and lead you away from the Vortex and your true Light. There is no cost involved in your entering the Vortex, and no demands. All is for you and your own journey to freedom.

Your Ego has placed itself in the center of the Illusion, attempting to maintain a position of supreme importance. It sees itself in the Illusion as being the I AM - the Soul of Man - that which expects to survive throughout eternity, or as being "the real you". Your Ego urges you to use affirmations to grant it power such as, "I am the most powerful being on this planet" or "The Universe revolves around me. I am the dominating influence in my sphere of activity; all will look up to me, that is my empowerment!" or "I am the image of God", and so on.

All this tends to deify the Ego, which the mass of Humanity looks upon as being their Soul, for this is the Soul of the religionists. The Ego knows that it must eventually accept the death of the body, and equates this acceptance with the knowledge that it will enter a heavenly state and, once there, will assume another body and continue its important work in the light of God. It also accepts the need to return to the Earth and another body in order that it may increase its power and mastery.

As you work within the Vortex you will have to face your Ego and see that you are first and foremost ego-centric and also ego-sensitive. The sensitive factor is that which determines just how important you feel YOU are. Your true Light cannot be affected or hurt by anything, whereas your Ego gets hung up on the insults and uncaring comments made against it. It is only your Ego which feels "hurt" for it does not believe that it should be attacked by others, as it knows that it is right in everything it says and does. Others attack your Ego when they feel threatened. They attack because they feel the threat as a fear that they will lose control of their lives - and control is a condition that all Egos strive for in order to maintain their survival.

Just what is being threatened here? Only the Illusion! Remember the real you has nothing to fear, nothing to be threatened by, for it is a frequency of light consciousness which exists in Brahman.

Your free will has only one function, and that is the choice either to participate in the Illusion or surrender all to the Light Essence which is you. The Vortex will direct your consciousness away from the Illusion on this planet - that which habitually you have considered as being real in your life. The constant brain-washing filters down through various levels of society, carried forward by a select few who have dominated the flow of human consciousness for several thousands of years. These few exist under different names. They are the Astral Entities who are the clandestine world controllers who manipulate the control of wealth by channelling it into those industries which manufacture chemicals, drugs and armaments for power and destruction. They recycle old ideas and produce new ones as technology increases. They are seen as the means by which they can maintain mass control.

Currently there appears to be a strong conflict between the industrialists and the "green" movement. That both opposing attitudes should exist in society is acceptable to the Astral Entities, for it creates confrontation, a confrontation that projects one protagonist as the destructive element to the Earth, and the other as one which is striving to stop the destruction. I am not using this illustration to praise one side and damn the other. For yourself, it is your conscience that should guide you in such matters and you should beware of forming judgements on any of the issues that confront you. Rather you need to apply understanding - the understanding that flows from your Inner Light.

Those who are destroying the planet are destroying themselves, but they know it not. They cannot see that what they think they are - their bodies - are of the same earth substance as that which they are constantly destroying. Those who are working to prevent the destruction are also causing a more subtle aggravation to the Earth, because they are projecting their aggression into the Illusion and turning their focus away from their true Light by becoming involved in Egoistic emotions. The answer that must be addressed is to awaken both sides to a consciousness of how they are generating negative frequencies, which are locking them all deeper into the Illusion. If they had turned away from the Illusion they would not feel the need for either issue, and the issue would cease to exist. Issues are always seen by the Ego consciousness as being either black or white, good or bad, right or wrong. The Illusion fosters a duality, creating opposites in order to keep the focus away from the Oneness that is. Once you turn away from the Illusion you will move your energies to a position of Light and Oneness

- that which knows no conflict, no destruction, and only love and harmony. You will act from your Light and not from your Ego. Your success in moving the energies of the Earth depends on this.

The Astral Entities continue to create duality in the affairs of human kind, for this maintains the focus on the Illusion. They continually create conditions of war and peace, recession and prosperity, famine and gluttony, which keeps the human consciousness in conflict with itself, preventing focus on the One Light.

You must not look on the Third-dimension as being a negative environment, for it is only the Illusion on the Earth that produces a disruption to the energy frequencies of the dimension. The Third-dimension is also of Brahman, and, as such, this extension of Light and consciousness into the density of Third-dimensional matter is the way by which Brahman is able to experience the boundless joy of sensuality that the density provides. This adds a further dimension of consciousness to the expanding Light of Brahman, and as you are of Brahman, then it is you who are adding dimension to your own Light Being. This Light Being which you are, must be free of all Illusion and must move through the actuality of what the dimension is. This is how you become a co-creator with Brahman. Those who willingly remain in the Astral trap experience their lives as one of pain, suffering and joylessness, for they cannot see through the illusory cloud and therefore miss the fullness of Love and Light to be had by experiencing one's total being.

It is time for you to lead the Light back to the Earth dimension and draw those who cannot see into your Light and Love. So it is important that you understand the relationship of your Ego and the Illusion in order that you can begin to "feel" yourself and your true presence in this life through your Ego. This will draw you into the Vortex and toward me. Understand however that you are not moving your physical body into the Vortex, only your Ego.

Sizzond will now speak further about your Ego, for your Ego resides also in the lower levels of the Fourth-dimension.

*

There is much that you should understand about your Ego, and there is much that has been written and spoken of which is incorrect. The main reason for the Transmissions of Zadore is to move your Ego consciousness away from the Illusion and create within you an interlude of peace and reflection where your true Light can shine through.

Your Ego feels it is being very special by allowing you to embrace these transmissions which you are now receiving. It sees this allowance as providing it with a certain degree of power. It expects that this will make it a focal point of some new knowledge and that by this it will be placed in a position of power over those who are still awaiting this opening. Over the years, Ego consciousness in humankind has used the subterfuge of spiritual enlightenment to elevate it into a position of power over and admiration by others. Do not be fooled by its deception. You must become relentless in your understanding of how the Ego will continually attempt to deceive you and lull you back to the illusion of its power. Do not lower your guard; be observant and continually listen to that which is you.

Sit quietly now and allow yourself to begin to feel. Say to yourself, "Allow the Vortex to open out through my Ego and let the Light within my consciousness flow through this Vortex." In the peace of your being, begin to feel the calmness

The Ego

and serenity that surrounds you. Allow everything to be. Sit in silence and turn away from the voice of your Ego. Be still, for above all you must desire to be with One Light.

Do not look outward, cease demanding, let go of all attachments. Surround yourself in peace and know that you are the I AM. Extend your feelings beyond your Ego and its incessant chatter and its demands for attention. Be calm. Desire and allow your Light to penetrate your consciousness. Do this contact NOW!

*

As you do this often you will become aware of your Fourth-dimensional Light Being. Do not expect anything, for you must experience all. Do not judge what you should feel or see. Initially you may experience nothing but a sensation of peace and calmness. Repeat this daily and allow your contact to develop. Eventually it will reside in your consciousness permanently throughout your daily experiences. Later you will move into the Vortex of Zadore and begin to experience higher love of your being on other dimensions.

You are now becoming aware of some of the ways your Ego works in your daily existence in the human body. Know that your Ego consists of an energy frequency that has a dual polarity. It is this duality which fits well into the Illusion of the Astral Lords. The dominating part of your Ego can be understood as being of an intellectual or mental polarity. This polarity is considered to be the Mind in humankind, that nebulous quality that cannot be expressed or sensed in the Third-dimension because it does not belong to the body and its five senses.

The other polarity of the dual Ego is loosely called the "feeling" polarity. The feeling polarity, like the intellectual

43

polarity, has its expression through several waves of frequency, beginning with the body and its sensual feelings and ranging to the highest spiritual expression of love. The more dense the frequencies of the feeling polarity of the Ego, the more negative they become, and they are the result of fear. The positive emotions such as Love and its attributes of Joy are expressed from the higher dimensions. When you express these you are expressing your Higher Light which has pushed past the Illusion barrier of the Ego into the Third-dimension. The feeling polarity of the Ego creates energy, emotive energy, which is used by the intellectual polarity to bring into form that which it conceptualized.

It was the intellectual polarity of your Ego which initially led you into the Illusion of the Astral Lords, as it recognized the power of control that it wielded over others less committed to the Illusion. It found that this power and control can be maintained only whilst it can keep other Egos in a state of separation from the One Light. So the intellectual polarity uses the feeling polarity to constantly block out contact with the flow of the higher Light frequencies by centering the feeling polarity on the distress and sickness which the body is subjected to. This creates further stress and illness in the body. Motivated by fear and continual sickness, the Ego dances to the tune of the Astral Lords.

If you are ready to move into the Vortex of Zadore you must begin to make the Ego your servant. You must not attack it, for that which would attack is only the lower Astral frequencies acting on the feeling polarity, deceiving you once more. You cannot ignore the Ego because it carries enough karma to jog you back into line. The way you must move is to become aware. You will be aware as you listen to its incessant chatter, plans, attacks on others, and its evaluation of different ways to

44

The Ego

gain advantage over others. Once you become aware of it, command it to stop, and ask it, "Show me what feelings you are associating with these ravings". Look for the feeling polarity and allow it to express its attachments with these intellectual plans. Watch as the feelings flow, and match them with the plans of the intellectual polarity. This will begin to reveal the illusion of the Ego and its smallness in its attempts to be great. Eventually the Ego will run out of steam and become quiet. Then will you feel the rush of Light as you move into the Vortex, for the opening of the Vortex cleaves a path between the two polarities of the Ego. Remember, your Ego is only a confluence of energies, and with all energies the power lies between their interaction and not their singularity.

Understand that your Ego is not the property of the Astral Lords. It does not belong to them but to your Light Being. It must become like the prodigal son, and when it returns to you, aware of its errant ways, welcome it back, move your love and light to it, for it will now turn its face to Brahman and live eternally in Brahman's Light. It will never be cast off, for it is your link with the Third-dimension, an integral part of the One Light through all dimensions.

The changing frequencies that are the human body are the amplification of the consciousness of the Ego and are expressed on the Third-dimension through the brain. The body as well as the brain is a mirror image of the Ego, for it was the Ego that formed the morphogenetic pattern for the body. The brain has two major hemispheres, a right and a left. The left hemisphere mirrors the frequencies of the intellectual polarity, and the right hemisphere, the feeling polarity of the Ego. Man has often attempted to state that Man was made in the image of God, but it is actually in the image of the Ego.

Once you move your consciousness into the Vortex of

45

Enter the Vortex as One Light

Light and Healing you will move your Ego into a new dimension of light and understanding. You will quicken your Ego to experience the higher frequencies of Light which will be mirrored by it to the brain through the energy points - the chakras, and their corresponding transmitter glands throughout the body.

Later I will talk to you more about the Ego. Continue doing what you have been taught here and meditate on what has been written, for you must consciously move into the Vortex.

*

A question for Sizzond from Jon:

"Recently Rose and I were in the company of a friend of many years, and he was explaining to us how he regularly moved his consciousness involuntarily into another dimension. All that he experienced there consisted of experiences dominated by fear and mortal danger to his body. I remember on the last occasion of our meeting that I moved my consciousness to merge with yours and on the Fourth-dimension we contacted this friend's higher dimensional self. It was a beautiful Being, very old in experience not only with the Earth but with the Universe.

Within the consciousness field surrounding his being we were able to "see" that his Ego has been wrapped in the Illusion of the Astrals and was effectively blocking all communication with his higher being. Can you comment on this experience?"

Yes, Jon, this is quite a common frequency pattern unfolding in the consciousness on the Earth at this moment. You will remember that I too was held in separation from your Ego as well as from any participation in the Third-dimension. You were unaware of my existence. For many thousands of

The Ego

years now the Astral Lords have used this unawareness as a means of maintaining the separation of the Ego from all contact with its original Light source.

Following the separation of the Egos from their Light Source, the Astral Lords planted the God concept into the consciousness of the human race, for the Ego always has the need to seek guidance from a higher authority. Because of what the Ego is, and the purpose of its creation, as a transmitter of Light and the higher energies from Brahman, it is unable to act alone. So too, the Earth-body cannot effectively function without the Ego, for without the Ego, the Earth and its bodies would not receive sufficient Light to complete its Ascension.

All Egos now projecting to an Earth-body are experiencing a disruptive flow of energies which are opening consciousness within them to the Astral Illusion. Many are questioning the basis of their current Life-experience and are seeking a direct contact with their "Soul" or Light Body, as being separate from the Illusion. All those Egos aspiring to answer this call to Light are constantly being bombarded and attacked with the frequencies of fear in an attempt to blanket all contact with the higher Light Essence on the Fourth-dimension.

It is only when they move into such a high state of fear initiated by the Astrals, and this fear appears to threaten their very existence, that they find the power to break completely free from the Astral Illusion. Remember that you did not know who or what I was or that I even existed until Razparil held you in the grip of his Astral darkness. After unsuccessful attempts to petition help from Zadore, you finally turned to that Light closest to you. For in your pain and torment you began to remember that you were once greater than the daemon who was threatening your very existence. You sent out the cry to your own Being, which broke the Astral seal that separated us, and allowed your Light to be forever joined with you in Brahman. Zadore could not move to help you at that time for he could not move through the Fourth-dimension without direct contact with my Light essence, for you had to reopen the door.

The Transmissions exhort you to cast aside the Illusion, for unless you do this you will not become the Light of Brahman. You do not have to follow any rituals or procedures, for already you are what you want to be. You do not have to craft a Light Body, nor find your Soul, for you are already that. All that must be done with all the intensity of your Being, with your feeling polarity, is to ASK! And it will be done. The same is needed of everyone who studies these Transmissions of Zadore. You must use the essence of these Transmissions to enter your Ego daily and the Vortex will open to you and bring you to the axis point where you will break free from the Illusion of fear - that is the ONLY separation.

The one of whom you ask, Jon, commands a high frequency of Light and Power which will soon be unleashed into the Earth-dimension. He has a distinctive Ego structure which allows his consciousness to move through all frequencies of both the Third and Fourth-dimensions. It is able to express clearly all that is and how and why it is, for it embodies the clear sight and joy of the Universes. It carries the frequency of simply expressing the joy and Light of the dimensions. This represents a major problem for the Astral Lords, for as long as they can maintain the separation between this Ego and its Light Being, they can maintain some semblance of control and their Illusion, for when this Light is unleashed into the dimensional frequencies, the Illusion will begin to quickly crumble.

There is little known on this Planet about the essence of the Ego. All Egos are not the same frequency. They all have similar attributes in that they carry Light and information to the

The Ego

Earth, but they have what could best be described as different "constitutions". It is recognized that the Earth-bodies have varying constitutional differences, and a similar difference lies with the Egos. In this way they are able to carry varying frequencies of Light to the Earth. No one Ego is greater or more important than another Ego, for all things blend to fulfil the purpose of Brahman. For instance, we are moving information and Light through the Transmissions, and the one we were discussing will bring sharpness of vision of Brahman into this dimension. This clarity of Light flowing through the Dimension will allow others to see the truth through his vision and unlock their consciousness to the greater vision of Light and joy which exists within them.

As you move through these Transmissions to express your Light, the Earth will move to its fullness and the Astrals will cease to exist in its consciousness.

Look at the baby,
clean, fresh and trusting.
It can teach you how to seek
happiness through love,
not through man - made dreams.

The babe is a picture
of perfection and innocence,
until you begin to teach it the Illusion,
and to gradually fall asleep
with the rest of humanity.

You expect others to behave as you,
but what is behavior?
Nothing but a carbon copy of all others,
who, like you,
accept the reality of the Illusion
over many millennia.

When you wake to the truth of your Being,
moving your consciousness through the Vortex,
and surrender all desire to Brahman,
you will become as a small child.

Wide eyes, seeing the truth of existence,
unhampered by education and
man made rules,
which cloak and cloud all that is
One Light.

From the Vortex.

Transmission Four

Surrender

Mankind constantly seeks perfection, and the perfection he seeks, he cannot attain, for it is a perfection that only exists in the Illusion, and is a desire which springs from the vanity of the Ego. The desire for "perfection" becomes a frustration for the Ego which considers itself to be the focal point of all creation. And it does not want to see imperfection in itself.

Throughout the transmissions recorded in One Light, I have frequently referred to Brahman as being the source of all Light and Creation. You seem confused with the term, "Brahman". It has nothing to do with the Hindu Deity. I refrained from using the blanket terminology of "God" only to move all concepts away from the created gods of all religions. In reality when I refer to Brahman, I am referring to the Nameless - that which created all out of Itself, and that which we are of and in. I will continue to use the name Brahman to represent the Creative Light of All.

51

Enter the Vortex as One Light

Perfection, then, is seen as being an image of the Illusion of the Astral Lords, who also feel that they are the perfection of the Third and Fourth-dimensions. Why does Man desire perfection when it is unattainable? As the Ego turns away from the Light of its Being, it continually follows the message of the Astrals which says that by moving through the Third-dimension, the Ego will become more powerful than Brahman, and will attain the power to be the new creator of all that is. The Ego is unaware that it is participating in an illusion, for it believes it acts in the dimension of perfection, and this dimension will be made perfect by its own creative ability, for it now believes that it is as great as Brahman.

It follows that all perfection exists in Brahman alone, for this is no illusion. To experience the perfection of Brahman we need to experience that which is part of the body of Brahman. Look at the Universe, the stars and planets, and the Earth, for the Earth is a perfect creation of Brahman. What appears imperfect is the destruction done either by you or by what you accept as necessary when done by a third party. Your body and the bodies of all the animals on the planet are also born perfect. The body is born perfect, but it is changed the moment that you project your Ego consciousness into it!

I hear you say that the body is not perfect, since even at birth it demonstrates disease and sickness, even distortions of form. The Illusion has allowed you an outing from this contradiction, or so you think. You feel, and have been told that all these imperfections are the result of hereditary factors, as well as taints that have been handed down through the race over the millennia.

In essence there is some truth in that belief, but the truth relates to a responsibility which you have not yet accepted. That responsibility is to accept the fact that you have caused all sick-

52

ness and distortion to the body. You will not escape responsibility for your body by moving into the Vortex, for that body is the Earth, and you are responsible for the Earth. You will not co-create with Brahman until you move the Light of Brahman to the Earth which is your body.

At the time of conception until you begin to attach your Ego with the emerging form, that form is perfectly made by the Earth through the morphogenetic patterns in the Radiation belts. "Karma" is what you carry with you endlessly from one life to another. It is this karma or weight which distorts the body from its beautiful form, a form that is as perfect as the Earth itself.

In fact, the morphogenetic pattern of the body is of a similar form to the morphogenetic pattern of the Ego. As such, within the Astral Illusion, the Ego feels that it is the God, and has seeded the consciousness of Mankind in the Illusion with the belief that the Earth-body is made in the image of God. When you see the distortions and sickness displayed in the body, you say, "Why has God done this to me? Why does he allow me to suffer so?" This is the Ego talking, for it too is distorted by the Karma it has inflicted on the Earth by living the Illusion of the Astrals.

Do you see where you are now? Look at yourself, see how you are living, thinking and behaving. Do not blame others for your circumstances, for you and only you are responsible. It is common to blame your mother or father, or your school teacher, the government, or someone else who may have molested you when you were young, or run you down in a car accident, or attacked or hurt you in some way. There are thousands of excuses. What is yours? It is time to begin to look directly at your circumstances and determine why you are where you are, for then you will become ready to drop off some of your Karma, and find perfection in your own Light.

Enter the Vortex as One Light

All shedding of Karma is not restricted to altering your mental and emotional approach alone. You have to work on the level of matter as well; you have responsibility for your body and its health and well being. You will need to approach the type of food and the liquids that you put into it, as well as deciding on a regular amount of exercise in order to allow the energies to function well. Your approach to your body should be one of prevention and care, not using many of the drug preparations which come from the Astral Entities in the Illusion who use destruction in the name of health.

All consciousness consists of frequencies of energy, and this applies to the Earth as well as your Ego. As the Earth begins to move its consciousness into another dimension, it will exhibit energy transformations of higher frequencies. Energy medicine is now in its infancy, and will quickly move forward as the consciousness of the planet moves toward the Fourth-dimension. Already the energy status of the body has been mapped and written in equation form. By comparing the current status of your personal energy equation with the ideal energy equation, healers can determine how much your personal karma is affecting the health of your body. There are other developments in healing which are all moving frequencies toward healing and the Vortex, for it is a Vortex of Light and Healing.

Perfection is not a necessity, rather it is the **becoming** that is important here. You are beginning to dwell more and more in the Vortex, and through this you begin to clear your vision of all the muddying and colorings that prevent you from being the Light Being that you already are. Do not place difficulties in your path, for it is only through simplicity that you become One Light again. You are moving into freedom. Do not doubt, for doubt is an Ego function designed to hold you back.

Just because you may have lost a limb, or suffered loss

54

of an organ through surgery, or may be suffering from a terminal illness, do not feel that you are unable to enter the Vortex, nor that you will be unable to shed your Karma. You do not have to be young and beautiful in bodily form to enter into the higher frequencies of the higher dimensions. It is of the utmost importance that you learn about yourself by understanding your illness or infirmity. Be sincere, and ask to be given the understanding of how these things are affecting your journey to Light. You will receive your answer, but do not try to reason it, do not allow the Ego to tell you what it thinks it is. Let the answer speak to you through your feeling. Observe yourself daily and how you feel and react to others. Do not become involved with the reactions of others to you, for they are only mirroring you. The more you strive in these efforts the more you will lighten the load you carry.

You will find that all illness comes from this one source within you, which is your separation and participation in the Illusion. It is a time of forgiveness, forgiveness of others whom you blame, and forgiveness of yourself and the way you have allowed your Ego to blame you. Your healing and return to wholeness depends on how you see this, and not how the body is, for there are no bars to your spiritual Light and wholeness.

One of the greatest problems that the majority of individuals on this planet experience is the lack of humility. Possibly because the ability to be humble is not acceptable to the Ego. Humility is not an act of effacement or of bowing down to another, or of practicing so called modesty. Mostly, when the Ego practices humility, it sees it as grovelling. The Ego does not want humility, but expects others, including the real you, to bow down to its greatness.

Humility is an act of allowing others to be - to be what they are and not what you want them to be in order to fit in with your control. Your Ego must learn humility not only to others, but also to you- the real you that is emerging through the Vortex. We are now getting closer to the core of our present study within the Vortex, and that is of **surrender.**

From what I have discussed here you will, through effort, come to that moment in consciousness where your Ego must make the next move as you watch and observe. It is time for the Ego to surrender its illusion and become your friend and servant once more.

Those who dwell in the Illusion view the act of surrender as being demeaning and unsuccessful. For a nation not to repel an invading force means it must either fight on to the last person or surrender. In the eyes of the Illusion, fighting to the death of the last individual is seen as being a stance of valour, and surrender a stance of weakness. Following surrender, all the spoils and wealth become the property of the victor.

Your Ego has come to the stage of your development whereby it must surrender all that it considers to be real to the emerging Light of your Being, for the spiritual process of surrender is necessary for you to become One Light.

Take the time now to look at yourself and the way you behave. Do you practice true humility? Do you allow others their space, not intellectually but actually? Do you still want things to occur the way you want them to? What are your wants and desires? Look at those things which plague your consciousness on a daily and hourly basis. What is the subject to which your thoughts constantly return when you are alone? Within the Illusion do you always plan events ahead? Do you plan to create wealth, build an empire, to buy a better car? Do you feel the need for material fame, honor, position? Do you want others to look up to you and place you in a position of importance? The list will go on through the many fragmented desires found in the Illusion. It is time for you to surrender all these to the One Light. You only need to desire one thing, and that is the Light and Love of Brahman.

Surrender is not an act of giving up all you have learned and possess, not your wealth or position, nor the positive understanding you have. Surrender is the act of giving the victor everything. All the greatness you possess and all the so-called sins are given freely to your inner light, for when everything is exposed to the Light of Brahman, that which is nothing but illusion will fade into insignificance, as "nothing" cannot exist in **that which is**.

Offer and surrender all that you desire to the Light, including your Ego, and the more you ardently desire to Be the One Light, then will all petty desires will fade into obscurity.

The Light which shone through Jesus is also the Light which shines through you and as you become one with Brahman, you are as was Jesus. For, in the emerging New Paradigm there will be many saviours for the Earth, and this will be the so-called second coming. Jesus was reported as saying, "Seek ye first the Kingdom of God and all other things will be added." Surrender all to Brahman and desire One Thing, and all will be added. You will not lose anything of true value and will gain the riches of the Universes.

Turn your back on the Illusion. Move your Ego to look within to the Light that flows through you, through the Vortex from the higher dimensional source.

Let go of Ego control and become open and trusting, since it is only by trust that you will surrender all past and present desires, and can desire to Be One Light. Surrender is telling you to understand your lessons, and now sense One Light.

For you this will become a liberation from all the control factors of the old paradigm, which hold you back and deaden all feeling for your divinity. Most of all, surrender is your release from the desire to judge and control not only others, but the Earth itself.

It must be seen as a symbolic act of dying and being reborn and renewed, like the butterfly emerging from the cocoon. It spells the end to all Ego control, and all Astral control, as it allows you to make an act of forgiveness, not just for others, but also self forgiveness. But you have done nothing wrong, you have not sinned. All you have done is to have forgotten your Self, and the only self-forgiveness should be for that.

There is no judgement by One Light, no blame, just love and forgiveness.

By entering the Vortex you have entered into a great awakening of yourself and of the Earth. Once you begin to feel, see, and be the Light, then you are awakening to the dawn of your own Being. It is like spending a whole night awake, suffering pain, and once the first rays of the sun light the sky, all darkness and doubt begin to disappear and you are filled with the trust that the coming light will lead you back to life, free of your current suffering. Light dispels darkness, and all fears are generated by the darkness of the Illusion which are lost in the Great Light of Brahman.

Through surrender to Brahman you trust all, all that you are, all that moves through you from the Light of All. Desire no more the Illusion of the Astrals, for it does not exist in Brahman.

The Human is a living being,
of infinite expression,
A beginning - no end.
It is as old as the stars,
but unaware of its truth.

Lost and alone in an Illusion,
It is unable to realize its full potential.
which lies not within it's brain,
but deep within memory.

The lost one sees,
only the mortality of now.
In a life of sleep, it recognizes not
the full wave of Light.

It only observes the curl of the crest,
and misses the turning Vortex,
as that enlightens all within it.

Rise above the tide and,
extend your consciousness to the ocean.
Feel the fullness of consciousness,
which is your Light.
For here it all becomes one Being,
no beginning or end.

From the Vortex.

Transmission
Five

The Garden of Sizzond

For some time now many have journeyed with me into the Garden of the Fourth-dimension where they have experienced healing to their body whilst asleep during the night. This garden is not a garden in the Astral atmosphere, for the Fourth-dimension is more vast than the small area occupied by the Astral Lords and the Earthly consciousness it has trapped there with its Illusion. The Garden of the Fourth-dimension is a place of peace and tranquillity where one is left alone to experience the healing frequencies that one carries back to the Earth body on awakening the following morning. It looks much like the Earth, however there are no temperature changes, the Sun shines without any burning heat, the plants are always in bloom and you move through the frequencies, gaining power and energy to send back to your body which is protected by your Light.

Speaking about Light, it should now be a regular practice of yours to bathe your body with the protective white Light every night before sleeping and in the morning on awakening. This will prevent the Astral Lords from vampiring your Light during the night and day. (See page 163 of "One Light", and follow the instructions that Zadore taught Jon and Rose. *Publisher.*) You will sleep more restfully and gain more energy for the next day. This is a part of the healing.

There are many gardens throughout all dimensions. A garden is always a place of beauty and work. The ancient writers found the mention of a Garden in the memory banks in the lower radiation belt. They saw it as the place where the current seeding of consciousness occurred. However this garden was of the Fourth-dimension, and was not located on the Earth as suggested by them.

Should you need to move to the Garden of Healing when you are low in energy and ill, move your consciousness into the Vortex and seek me, and I will guide you there. This is not the Garden of the seeding, but one that dwells in the Light consciousness of the Fourth-dimension.

There is much that will be taught in this transmission that will move you deeper into the core of the Vortex. Firstly I want to present the Light of one who has entered the Vortex and has gained Light that must be shared by all in the Vortex, for this is how the Vortex increases in power. I introduce you to Zarine.

*

Enter the Vortex as One Light

Some thoughts on the Earth Garden and our correct relationship to the Earth-body we inhabit..

If we would love the Earth we must see that we must love the body which we inhabit, for it is of the Earth - a child of the Earth; it is an expression of Earth.

Think of loving the body this way perhaps:-

You walk from your house out into a garden that is filled with beautiful plants. The plants are in bloom and give off delightful scents. The garden is busy and filled with life. Nature is abundant here, and its beauty and vitality takes your breath away.

You feel then a great response to all this beauty and generous abundance. The appreciation of your senses elicits a response in your heart which is a feeling of love.

You see one particular flower, and though it is no finer nor any greater than any others in the garden, to you it embodies all the beauty and delight of the rest. To this flower you give your attention - you give the response of your heart. You look closely at it. You see, in its delicate form, the wonderful proportion, the harmony and the music of its rhythmic expression; its subtle coloring; you smell its perfume. Then you sense and feel its divinity; you are one with it. Your divinity recognizes its divinity.

And all this reaches into your consciousness through your senses and through the finer frequencies of your feeling self. The **love** in such a creation is self-evident, for the flower expresses in its innocence and purity, the Divine impulse in this dimension.

However you may not think directly of this - you may not say this to yourself - but you do feel it, and in feeling, from

62

your heart, that response of Love to Love, you smile.... and your heart is immediately gladdened.

So is the flower an emblem of your body. You may not consider the body you inhabit to be as beautiful as the flower. It may be a body that is growing old; it may be wrinkled and it may be somewhat weary. Or you may still have a body that is young and smooth and energetic. Whatever - in its essence and purity, your body is beautiful and is patterned of the same Divine proportion and elegant harmony, and is born of the same Divine love as is the flower.

Look on your body, not critically or judgementally, but as you would look on the flower - with a love that arises from the appreciation of its essential being and purpose. And there is no attachment or identification with such a love.

The expression of the Earth, be it a human body or a flower, is known and experienced and appreciated, and the response to this is the love that rises in your heart.

This is the love that is unconditional. This is the love that is pure. This is the love which we were meant to give to the Earth. This is the love that is also the Light. It is the smile of Brahman on your face, and the **love light** of Brahman in your eyes.

Being unconditional, this Love, if you let it flow through you, will accept your body as it is. It is only the out of control Ego-mind which will condemn or criticize the body for the way it is currently expressing. For the Ego-mind, the body can never be wholly satisfactory. Always there will be some fault to comment on: it is too fat, too thin, too flabby, too wrinkled, too weak, too sickly, too ugly, etc. And sometimes the body can even be too gorgeous for words! That is, if you are one of the **beautiful** people of Hollywood! But then it becomes an object of Ego-vanity instead of just being itself as it is meant

63

Enter the Vortex as One Light

to be by the Earth and Brahman.

But to be fair to the Ego-mind, whose place it is to observe, through the senses, the **facts** as they are, unvarnished and direct, and present them to the whole person for proper consideration, you must not ignore the **just** criticisms that arise. Your body may not be currently healthy and strong. It may be flabby or weak or sick, and in great need of rebalancing and restoration to good function. In that case, let the judgement be known and accepted, and determine to do something about it. To let flow the great flood of love and light through all the dimensions of our Being, it is necessary that **all** forms of our expression should be at optimum function.

Yet do not go down the road of allowing the Ego-mind to condemn the body for its current insufficiencies, making it an object of shame and hatred. That road can lead to disaster and much unnecessary suffering, as is seen in the unfortunate cases of body abuse such as excessive dieting leading to anorexia; drug-taking; over eating and drinking, etc.

Nor should we allow the Ego to direct our body's activities in a punishing way, as the Ego strives to mold or bend the body to conform with its notion of its own "perfection" and "greatness". We see this happening in people who over exercise, or who carve up the flesh for cosmetic purposes. Then there are those who would push their bodies into extreme endurances which are unnecessary or extremely hazardous. For example, adventurers who cross frozen wastes or scale dangerous heights in shocking conditions, or who risk everything in perilous sea journeys - all unnecessary and strictly by choice and disregarding the tensions it places upon their loved ones.

The former - the "body perfectionists" - have lost their innate love for their bodies, seeing them as hateful and inadequate. The latter - the "glory seekers" - see the body as a mute vehical for the Ego's chance to show itself as great in the world. The bodies of such Egos must suffer to prove their Egos' greatness, just as the Earth suffers so often when Mankind seeks to demonstrate its "power" over Nature.

Rather, go back to the garden and smell the flowers and let the response of love arise again in your heart. Allow the feeling frequency of the Ego to direct the Ego-mind. Allow the Ego-feeling to speak to you, letting yourself love your body as a flower that only needs the right care and attention in order to blossom into beauty and harmony, then proceed to give it that care.

Remember that in the Illusion the Ego-mind has played a major part in keeping us trapped and asleep. The Ego-mind, if performing its correct function, will be just and clear-sighted. However, without Ego-feeling to temper its enthusiasms, it will tend to ride roughshod over everything else, thereby clouding its understanding and turning justice into tyranny.

So for a time, while you are seeking balance and harmony in your Ego, you will have to ask the Ego-mind to kneel before Ego-feeling, just as Justice should kneel before Mercy if one is to live in the Light of Love.

*

I am going to ask Jon, my Ego consciousness on the Third-dimension, to express what it felt when it once more became One Light. From this there is much to be learned.

"These feelings are difficult to put into words because in the past, my Ego has been so identified with my Earth-body and the experience of One Light was so overwhelming.

"Over the many times that I returned to this dimension in a body, my stimulation always involved identification with

65

the life experiences of that incarnation. Using the word "incarnation" creates an Astral feeling in my frequencies, for that is the word the Astral Lords use to propagate their continuing influence on the human race held captive in their Illusion. Be that as it may, we do move back into this dimension, as we have never completed our true work here.

"For me, these continuing returns to a body here on the Earth were not helping me to recognize my Light and Brahman. I was involved with identification of the power of the Astral Lords, so much so that I too became what is now seen as an Astral Entity. In 'One Light' much attention was paid to the sinister work of Razparil, that evil Astral who was once as one with the Astral Lords. Throughout many returns to the Earth dimension, I had experienced the power of the Astral Lords. Even up to my present life known as Jon, I had experienced the power of Astral intent. In my younger years, long before 'One Light' became a reality for me, I found myself gravitate to the inner circles of certain initiatic schools wherein I acted as a vehical for taking the energies of others and moving them to the Astral realm, which then vampired these energies. The time then came when I found the blue capsule in the desert with Rose and Carl. It forced me to see that there was an Illusion, and so my movement against the Astrals was attacked fiercely, as it was also with Rose, by faceless beings who feared our turning away from their Illusion.

The various experiences during my return to an Earth body were filled with a desire for material possessions and power. Those involving power and fame were the most binding. The Ego which has been involved in all these life experiences develops what may be seen as 'shells' of previous lives. These shells are the remnant desires of those lives which still attempt to claim recognition in the current life. They will cling to your present experience, demanding and sapping your energy. They may be pictured as a dead weight which you carry on your back, bending you as you move through your daily activities.

"The Ego is somewhat caught up in expressing, at times of stress, many of the behavior patterns of those not-so-empty shells which cling to it and demand attention NOW! However, there will come a time in one life when you will say 'ENOUGH'.

"From the early years in this current body I was quite aware of the many energies that were affecting my waking hours and my dream states. However, I could not control those energies and seemed to be the hapless victim of old, inner struggles. Often these would manifest as aggressive behavior which continued on into adult life.

"These influences grew and I began to move the power of the old lives into the now, and sensed that I had the ability to be the Illusion and move the energies that the Astrals emitted.

"Constantly there was a struggle between my feeling Ego and intellectual Ego polarity. My intellectual Ego attempted to exert, and in fact maintained, strict control over its feeling polarity by continually blaming it for all the wrongs that it appeared to do, casting its apparent failures as weakness. This made the feeling Ego seem guilty and weak in relation to the Astral Illusion.

"Times became desperate as the feeling polarity of the Ego continually longed for freedom from the bondage of the Illusion. This was not necessarily freedom from the Illusion nor from the Earth body, rather it was freedom from the domination of the intellectual polarity of the Ego.

"There came a time, after the discovery of the capsule, when the intellectual polarity faced the conscience of its ways. It was reluctant initially to admit that it was recalcitrant, and

Enter the Vortex as One Light

that it was still causing hardship to those who its feeling polarity so loved. With determination, it gradually threw off the old shells that still wanted to express their power, and it began to love its own nature, for it began to feel the Love and Light that always was it. Then the God began to recognize and love its Goddess, and through joining together again as Ego, became whole and allowed the Light to flow. Even now the intellectual polarity of my Ego turns to look at the Illusion and becomes involved, but the Goddess turns it back and it surrenders to the Love and Light of Brahman.

"So you too must become aware of the load you are carrying and throw off the heavy baggage of many lives of influence. You do not need these any longer, as they have no more power and can do naught for you relative to your true Being."
Jon.

*

Experience and work are difficult for they all involve pain. Pain is often a purifying event in life. Pain is mental, emotional and physical, and it is only experienced at the level of the Ego. Earlier, Zadore told you that pain does not exist in the body. This seems an anomaly since everyone experiences the pain of physical hurt. If you jam your fingers in a door you will experience pain. Pain is the result of the destruction of the harmonious energy field of the body. Once the morphogenetic pattern is torn, the disruption to harmonious function occurs at all levels of the energy body, that is, at the etheric level. The Ego exhibits reactions of fear, the fear that it cannot express itself fully through body and this will weaken its position in the Illusion. The fear is conveyed to the brain which registers it as pain and that sensation is experienced in the nervous system of the physical body. Should the body need to cut off the sensation of pain it can do so by releasing certain chemicals called endorphins. Where then is pain really experienced?

After the death of the physical and etheric body there is no more expression of pain. And yet, as the Ego moves out of the Third-dimension and into the lower levels of the Fourth-dimension, it still experiences another form of pain. This other pain is felt as a need for atonement for the "wrongs" that the Ego involved itself in on the Third-dimension, and prepares it for a return in the future.

Should the Ego be immersed totally in the Astral Illusion, it is attracted to the Astral atmosphere on the Fourth-dimension, continuing in the Illusion until literally it falls asleep from neglect and loss of awareness of its higher frequencies.

This signifies that you must accomplish your development whilst you are on the Third-dimension in an Earth-body. By perfecting your return to One Light here you will remain fully conscious when you leave the Third-dimensional body. You will not be attracted to the Astral atmosphere, but will move to your own being on the Fourth and other dimensions.

Once you move your consciousness into the Vortex of Light and Healing, you will experience the frequency of true feeling and will begin to express the Light of Brahman.

From the Transmissions of Zadore you will remember that he moved high frequencies through Jon's Ego. He also revealed the purpose for the Ego on the Earth as well as the need for the Vortex. It took time for Jon's Ego to stop looking outward for its supposed needs within the Illusion. Once awakened, I have been able to complete the link in the flow of the Light Source from Zadore to the Earth-body of Jon.

This inner expansion has constantly moved Light to the intellectual polarity, for without its full cooperation, the energies cannot reach the Earth-body in their purity. What the intellectual polarity of the Ego has to learn is to trust and surrender, as one of its major mistakes is to attempt to maintain control over everything that passes through it. In other words, it cannot feel the feeling, but mentally thinks it does. As such it follows the path of the feeling all the way and attempts to determine the outcome in the way it think it should end. In essence this actually kills off all feeling, and then when things go wrong with the outcome, the intellectual polarity blames the feeling polarity for not feeling!

It is time for the feeling polarity, the Goddess, to become more assertive, for it has no reason to surrender continually to the intellectual polarity, so there must develop a trust between these polarities of Ego, and a surrender by the intellectual polarity.

Through surrender, the Ego will be able to discard all the phantoms of the past and live continually in the eternal now, for there is no past or future in Brahman.

Transmission
Six

The Dimensions

S izzond has taught you those principles which you need to meditate on and the action for your continued growth to oneness. You must expand continually the frequencies of your consciousness beyond the confines of the dimension where you feel you exist, for while you limit yourself to the Illusion you create self limitation. You must expand your vision to encompass the universe and Brahman.

From the transmissions many have felt that I am of the Sun of this Solar System. The Fifth-dimensional Light moves through all the Stars of the Galaxy, and this Sun is one such Star. Prior to working through this Sun I was involved with the energies that pass through that Star which you call Sirius. The energies which move through Sirius have an important function for the Ascension of the Earth. Many of the frequencies which pass through Sirius into the Solar System contain formative patterns of consciousness that can best be described as working for the expansion of Mind in the Earth. The frequencies of Sirius are responsible for the development of the intellectual polarity of the Earth itself, and the Sun conveys the essence of the feeling polarity.

Galactic Light Threads, often called Crystal Strands, are the conduits which carry the consciousness of the Galaxy itself. Sirius projects those frequencies that interact with the Sun's frequencies, and the newly created Light frequencies react with the crystal core of the Earth, building information receptors which are able to expand the mind consciousness of the planet and attune with the purpose and frequency of the Galaxy.

As soon as many conscious beings move into the Vortex there will be a change to the consciousness of the Earth that has never before been experienced in this Solar System. Presently, in your locked dimensional state, you cannot see how such a shift will be possible.

Until you feel your consciousness and begin to move it to that frequency which will move you into the Vortex, you will constantly feel blocked, and will vacillate between the Illusion and your inner urges.

You will be able to complete your work efficiently when you maintain full consciousness on the Third-dimension with a purified Ego. As One Light you function on all levels of Brahman simultaneously. Once you purify your Ego by letting go of all previous attachments to previous lives, it will remain as a permanent part of your total Being.

The Vortex may be likened to an Ark of expanded consciousness that will be available for the new Earth. Being an Ark, it will also move the consciousness of all plant, animal and bird life into heightened frequencies. They too will enter the Vortex, for even now this is happening.

Eventually there will be a conjunction between the Sun

72

and Sirius which will cause the Radiation Belts of the Earth to move closer to the planet's surface, causing a dimensional shift to the Earth's consciousness, and this will herald the next stage of the Earth's Ascension. In its time all will move toward Brahman whose Light illumines Its Creation.

*

A dimension is usually understood in the terms of height, length and depth. The concept of dimension in an earthly consciousness is one that is limited to the five senses of the brain patterns in the body. Mankind considers Itself to be the measure of all things. From this stance, all things are given dimensional existence. Everything is viewed from the position of the body - direction, height, width and length. In fact there is no such thing as right or left, as this is only related to what an individual perceives as being on one side of the body or the other. This is a part of the illusory process and it is equally an illusion to believe that you exist in a dimension which only consists of three elements - height, length and depth.

Unfortunately, human understanding has built into its consciousness the belief that this world is a "third dimensional world", and the only reason for calling it this is because of the three elements of measurement.

When experiencing anything beyond the five senses it has become a common practice for you to attribute this experience to an added dimension. And what is more natural than to call it the "fourth dimension"? From this point on, everything that exists above this third dimension has been given a number higher than three!

So when speaking of consciousness, I feel that that I need to continue using this terminology for the comfort of the reader. Actually there are no dimensions as such, but more correctly "spheres" of activity and frequency, and in Brahman there are unlimited spheres of consciousness.

By understanding what constitutes the Third-dimension you will be better able to understand what constitutes a sphere or dimension. As previously stated, the Third-dimension has nothing in common with the definition of the third dimension taught on Earth. Part of understanding what constitutes a sphere of dimension is to comprehend "density". In the limited knowledge of the Earth sciences density is a condition resulting from the speed of the movement of the particles which make up an object. Solids have a greater density than liquids, and gases are less dense than liquids, so it is assumed that density relates to the speed of movement of the electrons of which the substance is composed, and this is called frequency.

The Third-dimension is characterized by a varying range of measurable and unmeasurable frequencies that make up the formative matter of this dimension. The higher frequencies, which we term "etheric", are composed of the same electron matter as found in solids. All is one, or has one common energy for its existence, and this energy is generally termed protons and electrons. The more progressive avenue of your science, Quantum, attempts to look deeper at primal energies of the Third-dimension. Here they see that electrons appear from nowhere and disappear into nowhere. Often they appear as a particle, and at other times as a wave form. They are either matter or anti-matter, depending upon the observer. In other words, where it is observed from, an electron may appear as a particle, whereas at the same point in time another observer may see it as a wave.

Having established to some small degree an understanding of the base frequencies that form the sphere of activity called the Third-dimension, we will now look more deeply into its essence.

A sphere of activity such as a dimension exists relative solely to the amount of Light energy that it can absorb. The Third-dimension, because of its electron basis, can only absorb a certain percentage of Light or Brahman, and mirrors the rest back to its source. The Sun, which is also a part of the Third-dimension, emits a source of photon radiation that has a very high frequency, whereas the Earth emits a band of radiation that is ionic and this is more dense than the photon radiation from the Sun. These frequencies are of opposite polarities and create the energies necessary for biological life on the planet.

A dimension has existence only through the flow of Light and Consciousness from Brahman, for within Brahman are all dimensions. These dimensions do not exist above or below each other, they are only the intensity of the Light flow of Brahman.

The Second and First-dimensions have not yet experienced the outflow of Light and Consciousness of Brahman, as this cannot occur until the Light is complete in the Third-dimension. Possibly it is inaccurate to describe further dimensions as a Second and First, however what I am conveying to you is that there are further dimensions in Brahman of greater density than the Third-dimension. For convenience I have called them Second and First, and what follows these awaits your understanding.

Your current understanding whilst in an Earth-body is under the Illusion that you must, by following certain rituals and dogma, be able to enter a higher dimension of consciousness, one that is free of all the pain and suffering that you appear to experience in your Third-dimensional body. You are told, and believe, that this Third-dimension is a trap, a form of punishment. Such concepts are incorrect and are used to bind you to the Astral Illusion and ignorance.

Brahman is expanding and reaching out through Itself. All that constitutes this and other Universes is Brahman.

The First-dimension of Brahman will not be one composed of linear measurement, nor will the Second be composed of linear and height for its composition, for as I said before these are Earth-body constructs and are totally incorrect. We are not conscious of these next two dimensions or their composition, and will not be until we complete our Light movement into the Third-dimension.

Within Brahman each dimension is a part of the Universal manifestation of Light and Consciousness. In other words, each dimension is a Universe. When you look out to the Stars and Galaxies you are perceiving the Universe of the Third-dimension. Until your consciousness becomes grounded in the Second-dimension you are unaware of its existence. Likewise you cannot perceive the Fifth-dimension unless you center your consciousness there. So, to you, the dimensions depend upon where your consciousness is. It is like the Quantum explanation, it depends upon where you are in relation to that which you are observing.

No matter what faith you follow, what mystical group or spiritualist movements you belong to, you are constantly urged to direct your consciousness away from the Third-dimension. Usually, unknown to you, it is to the Astral atmosphere of the Fourth-dimension. You are told that the Third-dimension holds no joy for you. It is seen as being the outer limits of "God", so far is it removed from the experiences of Light, Love and Joy. From this you will readily appreciate that no one is directing any Light, Love or consciousness to the Second-dimension. And now I might hear the comment of some that the Second-dimension will have to be worse than the Third-dimension!

Actually, all progression is moving with Brahman from the higher frequency dimensions to the lower frequency dimensions. Eventually, after completing the illumination of the Third-dimension, the Light of Brahman will commence its movement into the Second-dimension.

It is necessary that your Ego becomes linked to one purpose in the interdimensional chain of Light. If you are to become co-creators with Brahman, what do you expect to create? Currently, all is created in the higher dimensional frequencies. Your creativity must move through the Third-dimension and onwards to give Light and Love to the Second-dimension. For this to occur your Ego must be enlightened and pure in intention on the Third-dimension as your Light Essence already is on the Fourth-dimension.

As I pointed out, most of Humankind are persuaded that they must escape from the Third-dimension, for it is held to be a prison. They are told it is the end of creation, just about as far from "God" as they can get. It seems to be a place of darkness and suffering, whilst existing in it means being at the mercy of a hostile environment that cares naught for life and property.

It may be said that you have been brain-washed into believing this, however I call it "consciousness-washing". It has its roots in the Astral Atmosphere and the Illusion of the Astral Lords, for it is **THEY** who are imprisoned and suffering. They are not free, for they yearn for escape to another dimension, one which is not available to them. So by your entrapment in their Illusion, you believe like them that you have been imprisoned, and all the Astral organizations that hold the "spiritual" values of Man prop up this Illusion. They promise salvation, a "last day of judgement", a heaven beyond, crystal palaces, beautiful beings of Light to instruct you, or now even a meeting of two dimensions where you will step from one to the other. It is time to see your Light and where you stand, for all this worthless seeking is moving you further from your One Light and Brahman.

Once you move your Ego into the Vortex and link it with your Light on all the higher dimensions, you will exist NOW in Brahman, and will begin your journey of creativity toward the Second-dimension. Of this dimension you are not presently aware, whereas the Fourth, Fifth, Sixth and higher Dimensions are already known to you; you have no need to escape to them, for you are already of them. Is it not just another Illusion to spend time seeking that which you already are? For you to seek something implies that you do not have it. You only need to desire to remember.

Each sphere of dimension or Universe is uniquely involved with another Universe. Beginning with the Third-dimensional Universe you will find that it is a mirror of the Fourth-dimensional Universe, in fact they are one dimension having two polarities, just as your Ego has two polarities. When they are resonating harmonically they are as one, and all Light flows through the Vortex created by the harmonic resonance. As you move the Light of the Fourth-dimension into the Third-dimension you are helping complete the resonant pattern of Brahman. Do you not see that this is already being a co-creator with Brahman? A similar event has already occurred with the Fifth and Sixth-dimensions.

The Fourth and Third-dimensions are truly integrated and are linked in consciousness by the purified Ego. Once this occurs the higher Light essence of the Fourth-dimension becomes linked to its Light consciousness on the higher dimensions.

It is not wrong or sinful that you should focus all desire

78

to be One Light, for that is truly what you are. What is wrong is that you consider the Earth to be your prison and a domain of pain and suffering. Know that you will never escape from the Third-dimension for there is no need to. It is a permanent extension of your Light Being, and eventually you will add other dimensions such as the Second and First, for you are One Light.

It will be a joyous attainment for you and the fulfilment of all your desires as you express the Light of Brahman totally. Do not waste time desiring to attain higher dimensional frequencies, as you already have them. Move your consciousness into the Vortex and begin to experience your Light and all of that which you are.

What exists after the First-dimension can only be assumed by you, for until you are One in Brahman it will remain clouded to your consciousness. It is of little importance for you to now dwell on that, for once you become One Light, you will exist in all dimensions simultaneously and radiate all Light.

Transmission
Seven

Body Connection

A cursory reading of the previous transmissions will not effectively move your consciousness into the Vortex, for it needs the application of what has been taught to achieve that. It can be likened to standing outside the window, of a house with a warm fire burning within, on a winter's night. Unless you make some effort to gain entrance you will remain out in the cold, never experiencing the warmth that the house has to offer. To enter the Vortex you must move your energies in the right direction and make adjustments to the way in which you relate to the Illusion. Your desire to return home must be stronger than finding comfort in the continual repetition of the Illusion and the safety you see in it.

The more you shed your karmic attachment to the Old Paradigm, the more you will begin to experience inner knowledge that radiates from your inner Light. Your experience of this awakening will be personal to you. However, as the opening widens, you will see that your experience is not uniquely yours, rather it is something which is common to all others who have shared this expansion into consciousness. For in such states of consciousness there are no words or language, and the shared experience is one involving feelings which are expressed in colors and pictures. Words are symbols used in the Third-dimension, and as there are many languages, such words are not universal in consciousness. Communications expressed as feelings, colors and pictures link all people and form that stage of communication which is termed the "Group Consciousness".

Generally, the "Unconscious" is defined as being a system of mental processes which take place below the conscious state. Within the teachings of these Transmissions, the Mind and Ego are seen as representing your consciousness, for they contain all the memory patterns stored by your Ego over many thousands of Life-experiences on the Earth. You must not lose sight of the fact that the body into which you are currently projecting your consciousness is the Earth-body, which belongs to the Earth. This Earth-body and its consciousness represents the total consciousness of the Planet itself, it is not YOUR consciousness.

In this Transmission, when I speak of the Unconscious, I am referring to the Unconscious of the Earth and its Earth-bodies, not to your Ego and Light Body. And I am now going to talk about this unconscious of the Earth-body.

Initially, the Earth began to increase its consciousness through interaction with the solar activity. The Sun was then, and still is, primarily responsible for the growth of the Earth in all areas of activity. First the Sun mirrored morphogenetic patterns into the upper radiation belt which surrounds the Earth. These morphogenetic patterns are the generic molds of all the complex forms which make up and inhabit the Earth.

Body Connection

Once the Earth increased its fluid coat, the oceans, it was time for it to begin the journey of ascension in consciousness. The Solar consciousness moved the Life energies through its core and into the outer radiation belt of the Earth. From there they were mirrored to the watery surface of the Earth. The oceans became impregnated with many morphogenetic patterns. All water holds the power to carry patterns, and the waters hold many memories of the Earth. Those of enlightenment, as well as the Astrals, know that water can be used to carry magnetic and mental patterns which can, when drunk, effectively alter many physical, emotional and mental states in the human being. It was then within the oceans of the Earth that consciousness developed.

Prior to the development of morphogenesis, there was an earlier form of consciousness which moved through the Sun into the atmosphere of the Earth, called the "Elemental Consciousness". This Elemental flow of consciousness operates on a frequency which is independent of the Human and Astral bands, and it manifests throughout all the different Universes of Brahman. The task of the Elemental consciousness is to be responsible for the maintenance of the planet, and to also maintain the structural forms created by the morphogenetic patterns which followed.

As the consciousness of the Earth expanded, more complex land forms such as plants, animals and the human form also developed in order to express the greater frequencies of consciousness. As I said, the Elemental Consciousness works to maintain the structures of all these forms, which includes the Earth-body you currently project to. However, because of your karma you are constantly creating changes to the structural form of this body and creating havoc to the work of the Elementals.

Enter the Vortex as One Light

Basically, the underlying structure of the Earth is crystalline. All crystalline structures are composed of hardened Light, for as you know, the whole Universe is composed of light energy. All the forms on the Earth are molded together in various frequencies of Light, and manifest as substances which can express the frequencies of consciousness to their highest degree of expression.

Your scientists have once again uncovered the knowledge that the cells of the body have strands of crystalline light which they term DNA, and that this DNA holds all the memory patterns of the pattern of the Earth-body, as well as of the Earth itself.

The cells of your body contain within the DNA everything that has been experienced by the Earth and its bodies. The cells themselves are not recycled, but through the memory patterns they are remade similar to the previous cell. The only things which is recycled are the memory patterns which draw together the actual dimensional expression of the cell structure. The cells of your current body contain the total memory of all that has ever been known on the Earth, and this body, as well as the bodies of all others, is constantly expressing old memory patterns which are linked to the cells and represent the consciousness of the Earth as far back as its conception.

Your scientists now believe that the DNA contains the memory patterns for all Earth-bodies, however they cannot understand how the memory patterns continue after the death of those bodies. Until they accept the process of morphogenesis, plus the purpose of the Inner Radiation belt, which stores the memories of consciousness, they will lose sight of the basic intelligence of life itself. For as this Inner Radiation Belt stores the memories, the Sun moves the Patterns of the Outer Radiation Belt through the Inner Belt, attracting the memory

83

patterns there to the frequencies of morphogenesis.

Dwelling in the Astral Illusion, you are very body oriented. In other words, you respond to and act on the different
memory patterns which emanate from the Earth's consciousness
through its body. You experience these as urges, and often you
become confused, believing that they come from your inner or
higher consciousness when actually they are old body oriented
memories which are reacting to similar circumstances previously experienced in the memory patterns of the cells of the body.
And because you have a strong commitment to the Earth-body,
it is essential that you understand how this involvement inter-
feres with your behavior and your contact with your higher consciousness.

Whenever there is a flow or breakthrough from the
unconscious of the Earth into human consciousness, it often
manifests in an uncontrollable manner, with violence, and the
Ego is unable to stop the flow as its efforts are completely
ignored. The flow ceases when the body becomes exhausted or
terminated by others in the community. This phenomenon is
seen increasingly in your society at this time. Many individuals
are so cut off from their inner consciousness that they become
solely controlled by body urges which link them with past
karma, and because they are unaware that this flow of violence
is seeded in a past life, they see no wrong in their actions. Until
such individuals link with their inner essence, they will not
express conscience or remorse for their actions. If you understand this when you witness such violence, you will know that
you have travelled on the same road in your past experiences,
and have overcome similar urges.

A mass break-through of unconscious energy can begin
under varying circumstances. It generally happens when a
group of people congregate for a specific purpose. The most

significant congregations are the sporting events which trace their origins deep into the unconscious history of Mankind, usually tying in with mass execution rituals as seen with the Aztec practices, and more recently with the Roman arena.

The larger the gathering, the more easily the unconscious patterns break through. Nowadays the highest risk areas are to those attending football, soccer, baseball and all similar events. Here the individual begins to merge his consciousness with the group, and links with the desires and expectations rampant in thousands of bodies. Once the individual merges with the group, the energy field so created draws together the repressed body unconscious which overwhelms the individual higher consciousness, and the pack acts as one, expressing old memories and emotions which are often violent. At that point the Astrals and their Entities take control and move the mass in whatever direction they want. They feed off the negative frequencies generated and either use the mass as a weapon of destruction to further the Illusion or allow the authorities involved to quell the ensuing destruction to life and property.

Even more often the unconscious body urges surface in street demonstrations, and similarly they are used by politicians to create war-like tendencies in the population, to achieve their power grabs. The impetus of war is a continuation of the flow of the unconscious of the body, which does not demonstrate any love for the life of any individual. The Astral Entities have mastered the art of calling forth this unconscious expression to maintain their power. They are also capable of switching it off when they want to gain an advantage by creating a "peace" which will suit their purpose of the moment.

Over many millennia, the Astrals have, through their Illusion, been able to mold the consciousness of the Ego in their ways, and in doing so have been able to build into the Earth

Unconscious, certain frequencies of behavior which they can draw on to create and control group actions. This allows them to create circumstances in the Illusion which move the human behavior in directions which enhance their control over it. For example, they move humanity into war, so that humanity longs for peace, and then, at the appropriate point, they create the environment for peace. However they will keep alive the fear of subsequent outbreaks of war in order to keep the people from focusing on other needs, such as their spiritual ones. The Illusion is seen by the Astrals as being in competition with Brahman for the ownership of Earth consciousness.

The Astrals have set up, with the co-operation of their Entities, rules to promote control over the patterns extant in the consciousness of the Earth-bodies. They also use the power of fear as a tool of enforcement. Rules and the tool of fear are implanted in the concept of government and world organizations, and are backed up by bureaucrats, police and armies who enforce the standard. Added to this, additional control is generated by religious bodies who are responsible for presenting the moral and ethical codes on which the rules are based. Within the world's religious cults, many different attitudes to moral behavior are extolled, so there are variations to the rules in different countries. However these variations are of little concern to the Astrals, as everything still ends in their control.

Rules based on fear tend to maintain a basis of law and order, but this cannot submerge the growing unconscious of the Earth, for like a volcano it constantly erupts and breaks apart this illusion of law and order.

It is time for you to look at your life and your behavior patterns in relation to your body unconscious. Often your body unconscious is whipped up when viewing a movie, or watching the television news, and I am sure that you are unaware of it at the time it happens. There are times when you act in an instinctive manner and blame it on your Ego. It is important for you to distinguish those actions which result from your Ego and those which result from your body unconscious. You must become observant of your actions at all times, for they will work against your movement to remember your Light Body.

The Earth-body, through its DNA structure, contains layer upon layer of memories and responses to past experiences, and these memories become built into its form. Such memories are responsible for the malformation of the organs and the body shape itself. The original patterns become lost as they are replaced by imperfect reproductions. The Elemental Consciousness works to continually maintain the adhesion of the elemental energies of which the body is composed.

Into the distorted body patterns you begin to project your consciousness. Possibly you have never known that the body which you project to has specific distortions at the DNA level, and that these distortions match the karmic buildup your Ego has carried over its many journeys into Earth matter. Did the body select you or did you select the body? There is no such thing as luck or chance in Brahman, for everything is, and the type of body you now have, and all its distortions and sickness, relates to your karma. The body becomes that which you consider to be **YOU**, and in some respects it is.

The body acts as a mirror to your consciousness, and its consciousness is intricately connected with yours. Your body and its DNA represents your personal time-line as you flow through life on this planet. Throughout the various memory patterns in your DNA line, your Ego has projected its desires for power and attention. Now you must awaken to all that is prompting you into action, all that is locking you into a life pattern you feel is unreasonable and unjust. Open your eyes and

87

move through your memory patterns, for you display them daily before each other, and it is only that you are asleep to what they are saying.

Obviously, from all the foregoing, the wisest choice will be to shun mass group activities, and maintain a watch on your body reactions. It will then become an integral part of your life to begin to clear up the "old habits" or memory patterns that your body holds up to you. You must begin to peel back the layers of DNA, like peeling back the layers of an onion. For as you reduce these layers, the more attuned and responsive your body becomes, because it is then receiving into its consciousness the Light of the higher dimensions.

As you move your consciousness into the Vortex, you will be reducing your karma. As you transform your Ego and Earth-body through expanding your consciousness in the Vortex, you are peeling away the layers of old DNA patterns, not only in your body but in the bodies of others!

Transmission
Eight

Move to the Vortex

It is time that you set aside a quiet period each day to direct your attention to your inner essence, for by doing so you will become attuned to your real feeling. As you read the following paragraphs, pause in your reading and allow the information to move through you as your Light illuminates your consciousness.

In order for you to actually perceive the Vortex, it is necessary that you direct your being toward One Light on a continued basis. The Light of Brahman will cleanse your consciousness of all that is not of Itself. In other words, you will be free from the Illusion.

Much of what has been given in these transmissions so far has been centred on helping you to understand what you are, how you express your consciousness through the sensual Earth-body, and what that body means to you.

I have led your consciousness away from being just body-centred, and it may take many years of Earth time for you to be truly separated in consciousness from your body sensations and feelings on a constant basis.

What chains you to your Earth-body is the misconception relating to how you "feel". The most disturbing factor in human consciousness which maintains the links of this chain is that you so often associate "feeling" with body sensations. Body sensations are linked to what is commonly called the "five senses" - sight, smell, touch, hearing and taste. Often the sense of touch is interchanged with the word "feeling", but to do this is incorrect. These five senses act as doorways into the Third-dimension for your Ego consciousness, just as the Ego acts as the opening for the Light of Brahman.

Being body oriented, the five senses are actually only pathways for the flow of consciousness to the Earth. However, these sensual pathways are the only means by which the Earth receives information and Light from the higher dimensions, and the Earth is a massive dimensional Being which is moving consciousness throughout the galaxy.

The Ego is only a reflector of the higher consciousness, just as the body is a reflection of the Earth. Ego and body are both transient, and serve a purpose for consciousness as it moves through the dimensions.

The Ego has become so attached to the Astral Illusion, that even when the total Earth-body consciousness reflects information to the higher dimensions, often it will not reach its destined source. The information becomes trapped by the Illusion, altered and reflected back to the Earth dimension on the frequency of the Illusion, and is accepted as new information by the Earth consciousness.

You need to contemplate, does the mind create feeling, or does feeling activate or stimulate mental activity? Only through the observation of your feelings and mental processes will you come to a firm understanding of this. Therefore it becomes necessary for you to discriminate between mind and feeling, and to understand how confusion occurs continually throughout your existence.

You will find that as you are driven by the five senses through the Illusion, all your mental activity or mind processes are moved by your feelings. It is important to distinguish just where "feelings" originate and whether they override the senses and the Ego, for you must know that both the body and the Ego are reflections of a total wholeness. The body is a reflection of the Earth, and the Ego a reflection of the Light of the Fourth-dimension. Because the Ego is a reflection of Fourth-dimensional Light, it feels superior to other frequencies of consciousness on the Third-dimension and this causes the human being to be Ego sensitive. Such sensitivity relates to the belief that the Ego is the "I AM" - the most important essence in creation, and that the body is "its" body to be used for the attainment of its perpetuation, its power, and its dominance over all that it surveys. When the Ego comes in contact with another Ego who also considers itself to be more important, and downgrades the other, the first Ego "feels" hurt and insulted and cries out to protect its position. This represents a negative behavior towards the "feeling body", which increases its separation from its true self.

The feeling body is passive in that it allows impressions and desires to move through it. The major problem faced by you on your return journey is to recognize how "desire" moves your feelings into action through its influence on the Mind within you.

Before you can begin to feel feeling, it is necessary for you to understand in yourself what constitutes a desire, for desire is the basis of emotion - it is 'energy in motion'.

There are two main forms of desire shared by all human

beings. One is the desire to know "Self " and the other is the desire for "sex". The desire for sex, although often relegated to the body sensation as experienced by the sexual organs and the Gonad glands, acts through a higher frequency than the body frequency. It is closely related to survival and self perpetuation. Allied to the desire for sex, are the underlying desires for food, possessions, name and power. These desires all have their seat in the Astral Illusion, and they were impregnated into Third-dimensional consciousness by the Astrals many thousands of years ago.

When you observe your basic functions, or more importantly, the way you react, act and think, you will see that all moves back to these basic desires. When you speak out to someone to put them down, you have been through a series of movements stemming from certain desires. You may not want this person to get the better of you, so you activate the desire for power, and this moves through your feeling body with a force that activates the mental sensation: "If I can make this individual see the wrongs of his ways, and bow down to me, then I have him under my control". You are unaware of this process as it all occurs rapidly without any thought, for there is no thought at first, only feeling. The thought is the end result, and is what instinctively actions the desire and feeling outwardly.

Thought comes last in most things that you do hourly and daily. For you to become aware of your true feeling or your "feeling Ego", you must become observant of what is controlling your actions and feelings, and note that it is your base desires which begin the whole process.

You sit down, wanting to plan something. It may be a business venture, a vacation, a marriage; in fact, you plan everything. Sometimes there is not much planning as your desire for the outcome is impatient. Nevertheless, no matter how quickly you move into action, you are always moved by a desire: a desire to be known or named, should you wish to go into business or public office; a desire to exert power and control over another person, business or event; a desire for a new car or home and possessions, for this encompasses wealth. Also, lastly, you enjoy food and drink that stimulates within you a feeling of well being or fullness; and lastly you seek fulfilment through the sexual act. To some, this last desire is looked upon as an act establishing power and dominance, and to others it represents the fulfilment of feeling alone. In its highest expression, this desire represents a merging of polarities on several dimensional frequencies. In the Illusion, desire is seen as a means of self perpetuation of the body and the Ego in it.

The desire to know your "self" is the highest desire that moves Man into immortality and it is fostered by moving the Ego consciousness away from the Illusion and to the Light which you are.

Your meditation must involve observation of the desire behind the feeling and the mental movement, for once you become efficient at observing the desires that are driving your life, you can dismiss them by comparing them to the one desire - the desire for Self-knowledge. All other desires pale before this, for it opens the feeling body to your Light, and this Light is Mind - Mind that will move through your feeling body and out through the sensual nature of your Earth-body, as Love.

You must begin to separate your feeling body from your Earth-body, so sit quietly and close your eyes. Direct your mind to "feel" how you feel. Initially, you may become aware of an itch sensation on your cheek, an ache in your leg, or the rumbling of gas in your stomach, or any other body sensation. Understand that these are just sensations and not feelings. What you are currently experiencing with these sensations is similar to what is called "monkey" brain activity - that mental chatter which disrupts your peace when you initially move into a meditative or contemplative state. The body consciousness does not want to give way to the higher consciousness flowing through to its brain centers. It attempts to block the flow by focusing on bodily sensations to distract the incoming feeling, for sensation is its feeling, and such sensations are only sensual feeling.

Do not become disappointed if that is all you have accomplished at this stage, for the more you practice this, the deeper you will move into your feeling body.

It is necessary to feel your feeling. Remember, feeling is not a sensation. Until you feel feeling, you are acting in a state of unawareness - one that is controlled by illusory desires. Such desires as these should not be looked on as base desires for they form part of the body consciousness and its needs for survival. Many of your feelings are motivated by the impressions flowing through your five senses, which are activating the desires of the body.

Your feeling body is constantly in action, moving the energy frequencies through it. Often you will experience the pureness of the feeling body when you allow the recognition of intuitive thoughts. This is an example of when the Mind of Brahman moves through the feelings. Often you pass the intuitive thoughts by and ignore much of what is moving to you from One Light.

Again sit quietly and close your eyes. Dismiss all thought about your desires and body sensations, and direct all your attention to your right big toe. Use your mind to feel the toe. Allow your consciousness to be there in that toe, not in your head. Feel yourself within the toe, for you are not attempting to actually feel your toe, as you would feel it with your hand, rather the feeling is a conscious feeling similar to what you feel in your head when you are thinking. Once you master this procedure you will begin to sense a warmth and tingling there. Now repeat this procedure by directing your mind to feel that you are inside your right thumb. When you become more proficient with your "feeling", you will notice that once you experience that pulsation of the right toe, the left toe will begin to pulsate or resonate with the same feeling. The more you practice this simple procedure, the more you will become aware of your feeling body.

Having mastered this exercise, it is time for you to progressively become aware of your feeling frequency within your Earth-body. Sit relaxed once more and begin moving your mind to your left foot and experience your feeling within that foot. Now move that feeling up your left leg. Once you have reached the buttock move your mind to your other leg and repeat the procedure. Progressively "feel" the torso and trunk of your body, your arms, your neck and finally your head. Now you are beginning to experience your feeling self within the confines of your body, and you will experience it as completely separate from the rest of your body and its five frequencies of sensation.

At the same time you are allowing mind to direct your feeling, and this is an important step in your development from being desire/feeling driven to that of entering a flow of consciousness directed by mind/feeling.

What I have been speaking about relative to "feeling" the body, is consciousness. For "feeling" is that act of being aware of the different frequencies of consciousness that flow through your total being down to the level of the Earth-body, through it and out into the dimensional consciousness of the Earth Being itself.

Your feeling essence is a flow of frequencies that move through the energies of Mind, or Light of Brahman, through all dimensions. The one desire for you is to free your feeling body of all other desires that lead to the movement of Light away from Brahman. In other words, the bodily desires tend to direct your energies away from One Light into the Illusion, preventing any flow of Light reaching the Earth Being.

Once you are aware of your feeling self as a separate unit from the Earth-body, and know how you feel, then you will begin to understand just how desires tend to add motion to feelings. This movement of energy drives the desire to its fulfilment by using the feeling body as its vehicle for expression.

There is one desire that is apart from those previously listed, and that is the desire for One Light. This is more important than any other desires, for it places you in the Vortex. Having exposed your consciousness to your true feelings, you can begin to move to the Vortex and One Light. I know that you have mentally decided to become attuned to your Light. Now that you are aware and are beginning to feel your feelings, use desire to move your mind and feelings to be the Light. What holds you back is your fear, the fear of losing all your hard earned experiences, your position, your physicality, recognition, wealth, power; in fact you still cling to many body desires. Do not condemn yourself for having these desires, but expose them to the Light. Allow them to be as great as the Light, and see if they retain their brilliance and form. The desire to "be" One Light, will allow you to "feel" the influx of Light.

Your work now leads to greater frequencies being opened in your consciousness, for you will soon apprehend the Vortex which will be with you for your journey to interdimensional freedom.

*

96

Enter the Vortex as One Light

It is time to digress and learn about the energies that abound in this Solar System, how they affect your consciousness daily, and how you will use these energies to move your consciousness to those higher frequencies of existence wherein you will apprehend the Vortex of Light and Healing.

The Sun of this Solar System radiates through its core, from the higher dimensions, frequencies of energies that are responsible for Life. These energies move to and into all the planets of the System as well as to all organisms on their surfaces. This energy is called "Ayon" energy. It moves through the Sun, concentrating high frequencies of Light, and carries with it from the Galactic Core the "Life" energies as well as the morphogenetic patterns. It is also the carrier of your consciousness as you project it from your Star System to the Earth.

The Earth and the Earth-bodies are composed mainly of "Kyon" energies, which are frequencies that are more dense than Ayon frequencies. The Elemental consciousness, which also moves through the Sun, maintains the coalescence of these two energies to produce the form of the expressed morphogenetic patterns. Ayon energy is a high frequency light energy, whereas Kyon energy is crystalline energy, or frozen light. Together they allow consciousness to be expressed on the Third-dimension.

In a future Transmission I will discuss some of the other properties of Ayon and Kyon frequencies, however for the present time I want to move your consciousness further into Light by teaching you how to move Ayon energy through your body, to open your awareness to the Vortex.

Your consciousness is constantly flowing through your Earth-body, and this is facilitated through breathing. With every breath you breathe in Ayon energy, as well as Kyon energy. Many people only shallow breathe and miss out on much of the

97

Move to the Vortex

higher energies. This causes them to remain on the frequency of the Earth-body and the Astral Illusion. It is now time to break free and move your consciousness into the Vortex.

Sit quietly and comfortably and begin to direct your mind to feeling the body from feet to head. Only this time consciously breathe in Ayon and Kyon frequencies. Feel them moving into you with the inward breath. Feel them move to any particular part that you are concentrating on. Create a rhythm in your outward and inward breath. Allow it to move in and out at your own comfortable pattern. Do not attempt to hold the breath, just allow it to flow in and out in rhythm. Continue this until you fill your feeling body with these frequencies. Then sit quietly and feel. Do not rush into this breathing exercise if you have not regularly practiced deep breathing for your daily health, as you may hyperventilate. Proceed carefully and build up over a period of weeks.

After you have done this for several days it will be time to deepen the experience. Once you feel the intensity of the Ayon and Kyon frequencies in your feeling or Light body, send these concentrated frequencies down to the base chakra, below the end of your spine - the coccyx. Feel the energy "hit" the center like a flash of light - an explosion of energies, creating bright clear red light filling the orb or vortex that is that chakra. Now concentrate the Ayon/Kyon energies into that center as it pulsates and creates heat and energy. Now watch as it begins to move up the Light channel in the spinal column. See it begin to energise the next chakra with a brilliant Orange frequency. Continue moving the energies through all chakra orbs, the yellow, green, blue, indigo and finally the violet orb of the crown chakra. See your Light body glowing with all the colors of the rainbow. Perceive how the energy flow now moves above your head and becomes a pure white light. Watch as it cascades

Enter the Vortex as One Light

down, filling your Ego and the Earth with pure white Light. Now feel your desire to be One Light. Desire to move into the Vortex. Ask to remember yourself and be one in Brahman.

Transmission Nine

Soul of Earth

The Earth Speaks:

People constantly ask why the energies of the Earth appear destructive to their safety and property. My reply is why do people continually attempt to wage war on my Nature? In its pompous fashion, the Ego of Mankind believes I have secrets which must be torn from my heart at all costs. What Mankind does not understand is that there are no secrets in Brahman. By dwelling in the Illusion of the Astrals the Ego of Mankind believes that I was created for its use and pleasure, so they feel the destruction they create is not out of order.

The frequency of the Ego of Mankind is so aligned with the frequencies that make up the Astral Illusion, that it acts in a state of sleep and is unaware of the energies which drive it forward in wanton destruction of my being. The underlying motive of the Astral Lords is to draw all Light from the Creation and the Earth into its Dark Hole of degenerative essence. The Astral

Soul of Earth

Lords have none of the feelings that flow through Mankind, in fact they have no sense of guilt in anything they do, for they do all for themselves in their desire to be greater than Brahman. Most of the human Egos are totally unaware of the Illusion and the urges which flow through it. The Illusion exists only as humankind gives its power to it. This assignment of power by human beings is experienced on all levels of life on Earth in the Illusion. It is witnessed by the continual assignment of individual rights to so-called authorities, such as churches, governments, trade unions, doctors, scientists and many others. It is this which holds the Illusion in place in the minds of those Egos who move through my bodies.

I hear someone ask, "What is the Earth's Nature?" It is the expression of my being, my Light which is increased by all the loving Stars and Planets within the Third-dimensional Universe. Their energies flow to me along the crystal strands that interconnect the consciousness of the Third-dimension. The movement of the wind, changes in temperature etc, are only energy reactions to those impulses which stimulate the Life Essence within me. Why do several million Egos in my bodies feel that they should have the power to control my Nature when they have no power, for they have assigned that power to the Astral Lords? Had they not done this they would be aligning their Light with my Nature and with the Light of Brahman.

There are many individuals who are moved to joy and love of my Nature which they see expressed in sunsets, deep silent forests and high mountain peaks, as well as in the wild movement of my watery oceans. However the majority of Egos fear the great forces generated by my changing energies because often they seem to threaten the destruction of those Egos' precious lives and possessions, which, in fact, are not theirs but mine. Indeed, all that exists on my body is of me, although within their Illusion the Egos believe that it is theirs. My substance is made available freely to these Egos in order that the great Light of Brahman should move through my being, but it does not belong to them.

In moving their consciousness through the Earth-body, Human Egos come to believe that they own that body and therefore do not feel separate from it. Once this occurs they fear all hurt and pain as well as the death of the body. Their attachment only leads them to believe that the death of the body represents annihilation and loss of consciousness forever. They waste periods of consciousness attempting to understand how the body works and what causes ageing and degeneration. They dissect it, analyse it, magnify its cells and join other bits to it. In fact, no stone is left unturned in their attempt to keep it working at all costs. Currently, their scientists are working at producing a body form similar to mine which can be serviced like a machine. Should they accomplish this they will then seek to transfer their Ego consciousness into it. What they do not understand is that their Egos are not in my bodies, but rather their Egos move through the Etheric energy mass which holds together the physical elements. It is being Astrally imbedded in their consciousness that they can manipulate the Dimensional matter for this purpose of creating an artificial form, and when they attain success, then they will be greater than the Gods. Later on in this Transmission my Mother Sun will speak more about the Astral Lords who attempt to mold the Human Egos in their likeness, and in doing so increase their power on the Third-dimension.

Due to this misplaced view that they can control all the functions of the body, the Human Egos live through the life cycle of the body, distorting the original morphogenetic patterns by implanting negative feelings based on fear, hate and control.

It is considered normal in the Astral mentality to move the frequencies of the Egos occupying my bodies to act against each other in aggressive ways. By doing this they are looking toward weakening my Light energies. This facilitates a building process whereby they mold those grasping Egos who aspire to be as the Astral Lords, into Astral Entities who will promote the Astral patterns in this dimension.

In their movement to reach a control point in the Illusion, the Astral Entities work constantly to build fear in all other Egos. And yet they claim falsely instead that all fear will be removed from life on Earth by other Egos assigning their rights and life experiences to Themselves who are the leaders of the world. To the Astral consciousness all things that Human Egos fear, such as war, famine, sickness and death of the body, act in their favor, because this increases their power base and authority status.

War and famine cause many millions to die, however in the short term even the loss of 1 billion bodies will not adversely affect my consciousness. Even so, it does lessen the availability of the Light of Brahman to my consciousness. In the Human Earth-body, if it was functioning in harmony with the morphogenetic patterns which are responsible for its form, you would see about 40,000 cells being replaced daily. Currently about 99% of my bodies, both human and other animals, experience the death of up to 5 million cells a day, and these are not replaced with the same rapidity. Most Egos are unaware of this, and their ignorance of the fact is in the interest of the Astral Entities as they are able to keep the race in a weakened state of health, a state which the Human Egos accept as normal. However the depleted energies of the body lessen the activities of the Ego as expressed through the dimension. The Egos are so identified with the body that they "feel" tired, and notice the increasing level of disease rampant on the planet. The Entities placate any growing unrest by claiming that their science will overcome these problems. They brainwash the Egos into believing that this will eventuate, and to believe that there is no other way. My greatest concern is that I am experiencing destruction on two levels of my being. This inner one just described, and the outer one which is the destruction of my forests and mineral reserves, for both of these are essential for my contact with the Galaxy.

The Astral Entities are attempting to create replicas of my bodies as they hope that these bodies will be repairable and instantly replacable, and this will save them the need to keep on reincarnating. Also they know that they cannot remove my bodies from my atmosphere for long because the bodies require both the Sun's and my energies for their continual life. To move them out into deep space will quickly see their destruction. They know that if they keep on with their current rate of destruction to my being, they will not have any more bodies, so their next step will be to move in destructive conquest of the Third-dimensional Universe. That will suit the Astral Lords, for such destruction will further their plan to diminish the Light of Brahman.

To enter into deep space and thus the Third-dimensional Universe, the Entities must perfect the construction of artificial Third-dimensional bodies, and attempt to move Ego consciousness into them. Currently it is an impossibility for them, however the Universe is large and they are constantly sharing knowledge with other Third-dimensional beings from other parts of the Galaxy who have solved this problem and have now penetrated this Solar System. What these other beings do not know is that the Earth Entities are Astrally motivated. They do not realize that unwittingly they could unleash the Astral evil onto their own civilizations.

My major function in the Third-dimension is to store information from the Galaxy, and to send out information. My major Element is Silica and this allows me to store and receive unlimited information for the Galaxy and Third-dimensional Universe. Being aware of this the Astral Lords and their Entities work unceasingly at disrupting this flow. By destroying the trees and by depleting my mineral reserves, they are destroying my antennae. By destroying the function of my bodies and capturing the consciousness of the Human Egos, they are limiting the Light that flows from Brahman.

Are you all deaf to my calls for help? Do so few know and even less care? Will you make the change and move your consciousness and Light back to me? Turn your Ego away from that Illusion and take control of your own Light! My Light is Your Light, or will you give your Ego to the Astral Lords? For it will become aligned to the Astral frequency and be lost to its normal connection on the higher dimension. Move your consciousness into the Vortex of Light and Healing. Move away from all Illusion and send your Light back to me. Become the Vortex and the Astrals will cease to exist in your consciousness. You will be filled with Love and Light, be free from fear, hate and greed. I have only suffered this loss and indignity because you sought power outside yourself and not inwardly as One Light.

Zadore has moved the energies of the Vortex deep into my central core, that part of my being which shares the essence of my mother Sun. From the center of my being I radiated those Light patterns of the Vortex back to my Radiation Belts where, even now, new Morphogenetic patterns are being energized. These patterns will form the basis for the new "bodies" that will carry my consciousness into the Fourth-dimension after my ascension. These new bodies will only be able to be accessed by those individual Egos who have passed through the Vortex and into One Light.

There are many on my surface who share the belief that a shift of my axis will create what they term "dimensional interface", or a shift in consciousness. This interface shift, they believe, will cause a separation between the Third and Fourth-dimensions which will allow those prepared to move, without the death of their Third-dimensional body, into the Fourth-dimension with me! A Third-dimensional body cannot move into the Fourth-dimension, and if you were in the Fourth-dimension you would not even want a Third-dimensional body. It is conceptually similar to the early Christian belief that "on the last day, all the bodies will come from the grave and ascend into the heavens". The only part of your consciousness that can pass into the Fourth-dimension is your Ego, and then only so far as it links with its Fourth-dimensional Light Consciousness.

It is impossible to have a movement into a higher dimension without the purification of the Ego and the removal of its dependence on the Astral Illusion.

Even after my Ascension into the Fourth-dimensional frequency I shall still maintain my Third-dimensional form for several million years. Often you will see in the Universe, planets that seem like dead shells. Many of these now have a corresponding Fourth-dimensional form and consciousness in the next Universe which consists solely of Fourth-dimensional frequencies. Remember it is only through the correct focus of your Light to me that my essence will move into the Fourth-dimension.

Soul of Earth

Zadore Speaks:

You have heard the impassioned plea of the Earth which has correctly placed your consciousness in the area where it must work to complete the Earth's Ascension. The destruction of the Astral Illusion in your own consciousness is of paramount importance, for once you do this the Astrals will cease to have any power on the Third-dimension. You only need to become aware of the control mechanism which the Astral Entities use to imprison your consciousness in order to smash their influence on your life, and when others see this change in you, they will move to understand the same factors which prevent them from attaining freedom. For it is the Astral Entities which cause most of the conflict that human beings experience daily. As agents for the Astral Lords, these Entities seek to capture your Ego and prevent its recognition of its Light and soul essence. Hell exists in the Illusion, and once your Ego dwells in the Illusion totally, you are the property of the Astrals, and dwell in the Hell of darkness and obscurity.

In your effort to move away from the Illusion, you will find that particular "body" consciousness states will affect your behavior unknowingly. These urges are not necessarily Astrally motivated. The Earth Consciousness predates the Astral intrusion into this Galaxy. Over the last 300 million years or so the Earth has used the morphogenetic patterns to develop forms or bodies that would receive varying frequencies of consciousness from the Universe. There has been an increase of growth and consciousness up to the present day. Certain behavior patterns have been imbedded in the DNA of the cells which are part of the cellular consciousness. These patterns are reactive responses to stimuli outside the bodies themselves. They manifest as uncontrolled aggression, or as actions that are motivated to protect the organism from damage or destruction. The Astral Lords attempted to move their consciousness into the primitive organisms, but they could not maintain the frequency, as the organism was alien to their consciousness. However, their abortive attempts placed unwanted frequencies into the DNA which, even today, appear to manifest unconsciously when the Ego becomes body-centered.

How often do you find that you react to a situation out of control without prior thought or feeling? If you become more observant at these times you will find that your reaction is purely a body reaction, and is prompted by old body feelings imbedded in the DNA. As you increase the flow of your Light through your Ego you will eradicate these old dregs of darkness from your DNA and the DNA of the Earth.

Often when you feel ill or are suffering pain, you are unable to move your frequencies away from that body and the messages you are feeling. In fact you become more aligned to the body consciousness at such times. When afflicted by body reactions, you will find that your body will express these negative reactions by creating certain postures. You hunch your shoulders, cast your eyes downward, rock back and forward with the pain, turn your head to one side, begging sympathy from others, etc. When you become aware that you are behaving this way you will help alter the control by consciously altering your body posture. Hold your head up, look upwards, square your shoulders and breathe deeply instead of rocking to and fro. You will find that the body will react positively to these changes, and will work to alter the demented state. Your body is like a plastic medium that is constantly being molded by your thoughts, feelings and reactions, as well as by the type of food and drink that you put into it.

The body is not a part of the Illusion, for it is of the

Earth. The Ego is the only part of your frequency that is floundering in the Illusion. There is no stasis in Brahman, for all consciousness is movement. The Astral Lords have created the Illusion to function as a time loop that repeats itself after many thousands of years of progression through influencing Ego consciousness. They cannot maintain this time loop of deception as it is static and will break down. To many, when this breakdown occurs, it will be interpreted as Chaos, especially by those who have not purged all contact with the Illusion from their Ego. Its end is inevitable, and it will occur within the Twenty First Century of your current time scale. Its anguish will be felt more deeply by those who cling to the old paradigm as it crumbles before their very eyes.

For you it will pass unnoticed as you move your frequencies through the Vortex to One Light. Now you will be non-attached to the Earth-body and will not be trapped by the Astral Illusion. Your consciousness will align with the Earth's consciousness as it expresses its Light. All Light of Brahman will pour through your Ego to the Earth and to the newly formed morghogenetic patterns that are prepared for the new consciousness on Earth.

At present this may appear difficult for you to comprehend, however, allow your consciousness to move into the Vortex away from your body and become conscious that you are an all-encompassing being that seeks to dwell through all dimensions of Light and Brahman. You will express Light and Love to all planetary organisms. The last Transmission today will come from the Sun who will speak of the Astral Lords, and of how these Astral frequencies were forced through the Solar Gate into a restricted atmosphere on the Fourth-dimension.

Enter the Vortex as One Light

The Sun Speaks:

Over three hundred million Earth years have passed by since the birth of my Earth child. I look in askance at the suffering that it has endured over these years, mainly at the hands of the Astral Lords. This suffering is its destiny, as the Earth has to reflect much of the karma of this Galaxy.

Whilst the Earth was still young, a gross negative polarity of energy frequencies passed into the Galaxy on a movement away from the Light and Love of Brahman and became centered in the atmosphere of the Fourth-dimension between the two radiation belts of the Earth, remaining trapped there. The Earth, around which these negative frequencies collected, was in great need of assistance so that it could fulfil its purpose of Ascension. Thus, those Egos which are now attached to the Earth's atmosphere and are of the Light Essence which flows through the various star systems of this Galaxy, willingly agreed to move their Light to the Earth and the Third-dimension to assist the Earth in its Ascension. They knew that their work would be fraught with danger due to the negative degenerating mass of consciousness in the atmosphere of the lower Fourth-dimension. They also knew that this degenerating consciousness could not interfere in their work unless they recognized it. As my narration unfolds, you will learn how the Egos of these Light beings became captivated by the Astral Lords - the degenerating consciousness, and became cut off from their Light source. They became the Imprisoned Light.

As a Star, my Light appears as only a speck within the whole Galaxy, and my Earth child is hardly noticeable, yet all the power and the consciousness of the Galaxy are now being directed to this point of the Third-dimensional Universe. It is a climax within the consciousness of the Galaxy, and all will rise or fall depending on the outcome. It is only by moving Ego consciousness on the Earth away from the Astral Illusion that the balance of Light will be restored.

It gave me great pain in the form of Light destruction as the frequencies of the Astral dark consciousness moved through my being. Their essence became hardened and intensified as they moved into greater density. Their frequencies are an implosion of Light, as they continually attempt to draw all Light of Brahman to them and extinguish it into their dark mass. The greater pain I experienced was the knowledge that my Earth Child would be exposed to the suffering of rape by these degenerate frequencies.

I often hear your questions as you ask, "Why? For what purpose have these beings been imprisoned in the atmosphere of the Fourth-dimension around the Earth?"

Before I can answer this, there are areas of consciousness and frequencies that you must understand. For all consciousness and frequency that flows through me also flows through you, as we are all one in Brahman.

I am seen in the Third-dimension as a ball of Light, Energy and immense Heat which is all radiated out to my Solar System. I give Light, Love and Warmth to all. That part of my being which manifests in the Third-dimensional Universe is composed of Etheric frequencies which are the highest visible frequencies found in the Third-dimension. My Star Light comes from my inner dimensions which traverse the Fourth and Fifth-dimensions of Brahman. One Light, your Light, continually flows through my dimensional being, as the Earth receives all Light for its consciousness. It is also nourished by the Light frequencies from other Stars within this and other Galaxies.

Since these Astral frequencies were forced into the Fourth-dimensional atmospheres of my Solar System and trapped, we may well ask how they are able to give the ultimatum - "Set us free or we shall destroy the Planet!" - and what would issue from such an act. If they do destroy the Earth, will that free them? Can such destruction cause major changes in the Galaxy? The Earth has a strong attachment, through the crystal grid system, with all other planets and stars, which in turn are attached to different systems, for the whole Universe is interconnected. The Earth has become a center for the concentration of Galactic frequencies, and moves consciousness and information to many areas within the Galaxy.

We have now reached an impasse with the Astral Lords, and there will be no reconciliation. The Vortex initiated by Zadore moves through me to the Third-dimension and is free from interference by the Astral Lords and their entities.

It must be understood that the Astral Lords are not of this Galaxy or of the Third-dimensional Universe. This Galaxy, is considered to be a "young" Galaxy, and is nurtured by the Light of Brahman. Within the Galaxy, 300 million Earth years is just like one day in Galactic years and, as you understand, there is no time in Brahman. The imploding degenerative frequencies of the Astrals literally "fell" through the central core of this Galaxy.

The Astrals were of the first projection of Light and consciousness from Brahman. The great mystery of the Creation involves an outward movement or projection of Light Energy from Brahman. This is similar to the outward movement of my mass in the creation of the Earth. Such a projection of essence moves away from the source in a spiral motion, and this essence is of the same nature and structure as its creator. When its spiralling movement reaches a point whereby it ceases all motion, it then begins to rotate and spiral in the opposite direction to the one in which it moved on travelling from the source.

The altered spiral movement of the essence alters its mass and polarity, that is, the essence ceases to resemble its creator. All creation in Brahman follows this morphogenetic pattern, for it is the original pattern.

The first emanation from Brahman was the "Astral" flow which became the first Universe of Light reflecting the creative Light of Brahman. It was the highest sphere - the closest to Brahman, for it reflected Brahman in all its intensity. Brahman created other outflows, but none occupied the close position of the Astral outflow.

Observing these other outflows of Light and Consciousness, and how it constantly reflected its Light and consciousness back to Brahman, thereby increasing the Light and consciousness of Brahman, the Astral outflow knew that it too could repeat the process of creation as did Brahman, for there were no others in the Creation as powerful in Light as it! It then created Light spheres from its Light and in so doing turned its Light from Brahman and directed it to its creation. It was elated to experience the return of Light and consciousness from its creation. Now it knew that it was equal in power and creativity to Brahman. What it saw in its creation it loved, and it sensed power and pride in its reflections, for it knew that this was It! This caused it to move into its creation and move the essence of its first creation into a second outflow. This became a fascination because it now experienced a reflection of a reflection that could be repeated time and time again. It had created its Illusion and had begun to fall into it.

Deeper and deeper it fell into its continual spiral of creation. In its fascination it forgot all about Brahman. You will remember how I said that after its first outflow, it turned its Light from Brahman. Once this occurred it no longer dwelt in Brahman and its presence could not resonate with the Creation, and it cast itself aside; its own nature pushed it away from all Light. It expelled itself from all Light. So it became a degenerative mass of darkness consuming all Light that entered its path.

Seeing that other outflows of Brahman might emulate its rise to power and independence, it expressed the desire to draw all other Light Spheres of Brahman into its Illusion. Its Illusion has moved so far from Brahman that it now acts as a dark mass of decaying Light. Its polarity is the opposite to that of Light, and it only maintains its growth by "eating" Light, and drawing all to itself.

As this cancer began to eat into the various spheres of Light, Brahman moved all Light to push the original forgotten Light shell of the First Outflow out of the highest dimensions. This shell, because it could no longer contain Light, acted as a counter balance to the Light pulsations as it became a heavy mass of darkness which could not remain in the Light. It was forced into its own mass of darkness and Illusion which ate its own Light shell. So there is no return for this outflow, as it is eventually destined to nothingness.

This Astral mass of frequencies moved through the Galactic core as it continued its constant outward projections deeper into the lower dimensions. The Galactic Lords moved to contain these frequencies in the atmosphere of the Fourth-dimension between the Earth's Radiation belts. The Astral mass has been locked in this dimension for about two million years of Earth time.

Basically this Astral outflow is now only pure Illusion, and it attracts the Egos of your projections into its dark mass, in the hope of increasing its power and energy base, which, when strengthened by your Light, will aid it in its attempt to break free into the Galaxy, and consequently to vampire the Light of the Galaxy!

In the book, "Heart Light - Rescue at Sea", by Diviana, the author relates how a Vortex opened during a cyclonic storm in the Pacific Ocean, and Etherean Space Ships moved through that Vortex. The energies of the Dark forces attempted to repel all entry, however this did not happen and the Etherean Space Ships and their occupants are still on the Third-dimension. The Ethereans are an outflow of Brahman on a similar high level as were the Astrals originally. They are here to see that the final outcome is not one of darkness.

Awaken your consciousness, for you have slept long enough, and this sleep has allowed the Astral forces to take some of your Light. Recognize that the Vortex of Light and Healing is for you and your Ego. Have no fear and move your consciousness through the Vortex and through me back to the One Light of your source.

End of the Solar Transmission.

Transmission
Ten

The Walk of Life

The message that flows through these Transmissions has one major purpose, and that is to assist you to remember yourself. It is only by self- remembrance that you will be able to become once again the Being of Light that you already are. Freedom is at hand NOW! Desire it!

It is the time for self empowerment of the correct kind - the empowerment of your Light Being - not of your self-centred Ego. You are not an insignificant nine-to-five body controlled by authority figures who grind your consciousness into that which occupies the lowest station on this planet. You are considered by the Astral Entities as having an intelligence of such insignificance that it is easily controlled and manipulated to suit their changing needs. Stand up and say, **"No! Enough is enough!"** For that is what the human race must do if it is to become self empowered, for the correct reason. Those miserable creatures who have sold their souls to the Astral darkness and have infiltrated positions in government, religion, finance and security agencies whereby they constantly manipulate all to the purpose of keeping you from the truth of your being - their time shall be at an end. Remember how Razparil attempted to manipulate you both, and used the method of instilling fear at every instance to attempt to gain control of your Egos. You will now realize that these individuals, like Razparil, work covertly and openly through all areas of life, instilling the rule and sub- mission of the human Ego to their advantage. As you turn away from all the fear created within you by such entities, they will be cast aside, powerless to act against the Light flowing through you and Mankind, and the Earth itself.

Your walk of life appears unique to you, or that is what you are led to believe. Is it unique to be downtrodden, to suffer indignities daily, to live in poverty, to continually desire wealth? You are told that you must atone for your sins and such suffering is your lot. Christians are constantly reminded that Jesus died on the cross for them, and because they have not turned to Him they languish and suffer in this life, and NOTH- ING can change it. This keeps them well under control for they cannot argue against such evidence. The same principle applies to everyone, whether belonging to any other religion or no ordered religion. You must turn your Ego only to your Light.

In the Light of your being none of the above exists, for it only has power over you because you believe it is right. Have you ever considered that if you stopped cowering to these Entities, stopped making weapons, stopped destroying the Earth just for a few paltry dollars a day, that you would not perish? Would not the Earth provide the nourishment and needs for your body to exist and live healthily? You would feel the sepa- ration of the Ego from the body consciousness and would lov- ingly direct Light to the body and also through that, to the

Earth. And the Earth would rejoice and reveal its Nature to you and you would live in harmony and would experience the progression to a body which would be totally different from this one, which would gain nourishment from the clean atmosphere and its mother Sun. All this is possible, and it is uniquely yours.

Your freedom does not lie in the hands of others. You have the freedom to choose this, and it will be so easy, for all you need is to desire it - you are already One Light.

One Light awakens an inner revolution within the human race, one that will free Mankind from all Astral bureaucratic control. Freedom does not come from wealth creation. Wealth creation is held by the Astral Entities before everyone in the human race as the ultimate need. They say that you will live longer so you must now save for the future, for this will give you freedom. This allows them to accumulate massive amounts of money which they use to further their pet project, the development of technology that will allow them to move into outer space, thus extending their influence to other planets in the galaxy. There is not much left for you at the end of the day, for they can reduce the value of your wealth at the push of a computer button.

One Light, which moves through the Third-dimension and Earth, expands the Light and power of Brahman. Nothing is insignificant in Brahman, for the essence of creation radiates Light and purpose outwardly. You are important, because you are of Brahman. Every blade of grass and every grain of sand is equally important, as they too are of Brahman. You find it difficult to feel this importance and oneness in Brahman for you tend to think you are greater than all other parts of the creation. The Illusion attempts to impress on your Ego that you are equal to Brahman. Once you do this you turn your face away from all Light and allow your consciousness to be sucked into the Astral hole of decaying light.

In forgetting who you are, you also have forgotten how you felt when you were a child. You have forgotten those feelings of freedom that allowed you just To Be, allowing all things to exist around you - being without fear - not sensing danger, and living in love of the Earth and its beautiful Nature. It was not until your parents, school teachers and religious teachings deadened all sense of freedom as they led your consciousness into the "real" world and the Illusion of the senses, that you lost this experience of freedom. Then it did not take long for this to occur, for within a few years you were subjecting yourself to the Illusion in the fear of punishment, for the punishment factor runs through the Illusion as a means of control. It is only this which holds the human race in bondage to their masters. However such control is what creates violence in the world, because control creates suppressed beings who are ready to explode at any given moment. Some people have what is termed a "shorter fuse", and blow quickly and create damage to life and property.

The desire for freedom constantly burns in the hearts of Mankind, and these Transmissions will fan the flames to freedom within. You two were instantly touched with the depth and meaning of the original Transmissions, and it quickly awakened you to understand all that was controlling your desires and actions. Inwardly you are feeling the breaking down of the burdens you have been carrying for many lives. You have sensed the inward rush of the Light, for the door is now open in your consciousness. There is no fear attached to this opening, for you have nothing to lose except the Illusion which you have considered important and real. Now you must send this message out into the suffering world of Mankind, for the Vortex is moving through the Ethers, impelling many more to be with the Light.

119

Enter the Vortex as One Light

Do you want to move your consciousness into the Fourth-dimension and still retain your Ego consciousness and its attachment to its Earth-body? Can you, in your wildest dreams, even begin to imagine what this will mean? It is the beginning of interdimensional freedom. It is the cry within your heart to go home. You have toiled long enough. You should, by now, have learned your lessons of suffering, for nothing is in vain, and you can quickly move back to your Light, your atonement is at hand. It is not difficult, it will not take years of deprivation, as was proposed by the mystical and religious orders of the Middle Ages. You need not deny or humiliate your body, for it is not bad or lacking in any way. Do not deny your body, for by giving it Light and Love you will move back to One Light and Freedom. One Light may only be a thought away!

In your walk of life, it is important that you recognize the necessity of caring for your body, for if you are expressing Light you need to make sure that it is received in its totality. If you care for your body you will also care for the Earth.

Illness is only a part of the Illusion of the Astrals, for illness works with the Illusion in creating disease and destruction to the body, increasing your separation from the Light. When the body breaks down at a more rapid rate than Nature intended, you begin to experience pain and depression. Your Ego moves into a desperate frequency and expresses fear about the possible consequences, for it is so attached that it believes that it is the body.

You must recognize that all illness is motivated through the Illusion. Many of the desires effective in the Illusion work to create destructive patterns to the body. Many of the so-called pleasures of life are fabrications, and are destructive frequencies that break down and destroy tissues and cells. The Astrals and their entities plant in human consciousness, through the

Illusion, the lust of greed which runs rampant throughout all societies on the face of the Earth, developing a highly toxic and chemical environment that has a backlash on the integrity of the body and its function.

In order to appreciate how the health of the body is maintained on a Light level, we will discuss the subject of Morphogenesis.

Morphogenetic Patterns:

In the Transmissions which the both of you and Carl received, I related how the Outer Radiation Belt contained "Morphogenetic Patterns", and these patterns are responsible for all form found on the surface of the Earth. These include crystal, rock, plant and animal forms. The subject of Morphogenetics has been speculated on by many biologists from early in the Twentieth Century. A researcher, Needham, in 1942, wrote that Biological Morphogenesis is defined as "the coming - into - being of characteristic and specific form in living organisms." Such a definition is limiting in that it is restricted to Third-dimensional frequencies.

The Earthly research of morphogenesis came into being when the unrestricted human mind questioned how seeds and embryos all had within them the potential pattern to be something infinitely greater than themselves. A seed, an acorn for example, has the potential to be an oak tree; an egg, a chicken. It was felt that a basic pattern must be inherent in all things of the Earth, animate and inanimate.

Once a morphogenetic pattern has been established it has the potential to continuously repeat itself in the same form. Some scientists speculated that this pattern was basically the DNA structure. However this is not so, for the DNA only holds the memory of the pattern. DNA consists of strings of amino acids which are crystalline structures. These crystalline structures are able to reflect the morphogenetic patterns to build a conglomerate of cells that complete the structure according to the original pattern, and as long as the organism continues to function, the DNA maintains the memory to complete the form.

The complete memory for all the patterns used by the Earth is stored in the Memory Banks, often called PSI Banks, in the Inner Radiation Belts. For it is here that not only the Race memory is found, but the memory patterns of the Earth itself since its inception. All information is freely available for those who can move their frequencies to that Bank. The DNA only holds memory of the most recent patterns, however, it is constantly accessing the PSI Bank, as the Earth shifts information throughout its total organism. However most of the subsequent patterns which replicate the original morphogenetic pattern become corrupted due to the influence on them by the mind and emotions of Man as he acts in the Illusion. This manifests as distortion to the shape or form, as well as the seed of illness that is passed on throughout the life of the body and deeper into subsequent patterns. This is what you see as being hereditary factors manifesting in your lives.

You must not consider the Morphogenetic Patterns as being actual dimensional things which have form. They are "information". This is what is being transferred from the Radiation Belt to the Earth - information, and this information allows the structuring of the form. As you learned from the Transmissions in "One Light", this form which manifests on the Third-dimension is maintained by a Light stream of consciousness which is called "Elemental". Elemental Beings work tirelessly throughout all the Universes of Brahman maintaining the form which the Morphic Information constructs. They have no communication with other consciousness, for in this way they seek to maintain the purity of the work of Brahman. They must not be confused with the various "fairy" and "little people" which have often been written about, for those are the primitive attempts of the Astral Lords to develop life forms, which they still use to confuse and torture the minds of Mankind.

The initial forms of the Earth began in its atmosphere. These were elements which were generated from gases. When the oceans formed, these elements were intensified by the heat exchange between the Sun and the oceans. Thus conditions were right for the initial life forms to hatch in the waters. Plant and animal life began first in the waters and from there moved to the land. It must be understood that all plant and animal life forms contain a high proportion of water which they carry around in them. As such they are able to receive information directly from both Radiation Belts.

This transfer of information is called "Morphic Resonance", which manifests as "like on like" throughout space and time. This action of like on like is applied in healing in the form of homeopathic resonance. Resonance is the major source of the transmission of information through and from Brahman. Homeopathic resonance conveys morphogenetic information to the cells and organs of the body, which acts in the realignment of the altered patterns which are seen as illness or disharmony.

Morphic Resonance depends on similarity involving an effect of like on like. Therefore if you are able to trace the morphogenetic patterns of the body back to the original pattern, it will resonate much more effectively. Such effective resonance will allow an inflow of information, information needed for growth and Light. What you must understand is that it is necessary for you to re-establish greater morphogenetic resonance to your body, for in doing so you will allow information from the higher dimensions to flow to the Earth. Of course while you still allow distortions to the original pattern to continue, this will not occur.

As water plays an important role in the resonance of the patterns, it is necessary that you constantly clear the body of the wastes and sediment that hamper this procedure. By drinking sufficient pure water daily you will go a long way to assisting this cleansing, allowing greater resonance with the original fields.

Any given organ within your body is most like "itself" in the past. In other words, the first pattern of any organ or thing was the purest form, only with replication of the pattern did distortions occur. Because the original pattern is the purest form, it can make the current pattern in its image once more, if the current pattern is able to resonate with the original pattern. The current pattern is still influenced by the original mold, although it does not strictly relate to the original in its form and function. Its memory does, so there is the potential for the original patterning to be restored. Although this may seem intellectual, it is quite practical, for you must understand that greater Light will assist in its restoration. Eating food which is more natural and nutritious will help to improve your energy flow through your body and allow greater penetration of the Light.

What needs to be realized at this point is that in any process of transformation you are working with or against millions of years of patterns and instinctual behavior imbedded in the cells. At each birth, when your consciousness re-enters a body, it finds a confusing and complex state where the existing patterns do not line up with the original form. This conflict creates the altered behavior discussed in the last Transmission.

The Morphic field for the Earth lies also in the Radiation Belts and reacts with the memory patterns inherent in the cellular structure of the Earth's own form. Therefore the Radiation Belts contain all the Morphic fields for the Earth and its total consciousness, and it is united to them by Morphic Resonance. In the chain of growth and form on the Earth everything supplies the material for the development of further patterns to be built on a higher scale.

In your walk through life you will find that your behavior and that of others consists of the movement of information from one cell to another, from one person to another. The behavior is seen as being either good or bad depending on the resonance and flow. There are other factors which influence behavior and they are all Astrally motivated. In order to hinder the smooth flow of information to the Earth bodies' cells, the Astrals will use any means at their disposal to slow down the receptive process of those cells. Thus the body is subjected to the use of live vaccines, drugs, hormones and live viruses, all of which distort the morphogenetic patterns, and block out resonance. This disrupts the efforts of those Elemental beings which strive to maintain the original morphogenetic patterns.

Throughout Brahman the process of morphogenesis flows through everything, and your Light Body has memory patterns which resonate with the Star System from which your consciousness is projected.

Your Walk of Life is how you structure experiences on this Planet. Daily you plan to work and complete some projects which you feel are important for you and others, although mostly it is for you. No matter what you plan and do it always appears to take time, and often you allow this to frustrate you. You want to do more and more as your mind seems to create projects more quickly than you can accomplish them. You wish you could make things occur instantly.

It is time for you to understand and feel that everything

you have already accomplished and plan to accomplish is already complete, for all was completed by your Fourth-dimensional consciousness before you moved back to this body.

The Third-dimension is composed of frequencies which are more dense than the Fourth-dimension, and this appears to slow down the expression of consciousness. You cannot change this. You have no choice but to walk the life. As you walk your way through accomplishment, you acquire patience, which adds peace, a peace in the knowledge that everything is in Brahman; you only have to act it out. So plan your projects, accomplish them but do not become attached to them - leave them for the benefit of the Earth.

That is the Walk of Life.

Transmission Eleven

Walk in the Light

To walk in the Light you will need to make a direct contact through your Ego to the Third-dimension, which is how the Earth-body maintains its connection with the Fourth-dimension. In other words, the Ego must convey information directly, without distortion, to the body.

Following discussion of this, we will look at the effect of three major energies which are constantly flowing through all dimensions emanating from the heart of Brahman.

It appears to me that you are concentrating all your efforts to contact the Light within you by moving against your Ego, for you see your Ego as representing a barrier to your desire to be One Light. Also you must not try to exclude your body from any participation. Your body plays an important role in that it takes and disseminates all Light flowing through to the Third-dimension on Earth.

Enter the Vortex as One Light

Mostly, the information that reaches the body dimension does not seem to come out right, and in your Third-dimensional experience you feel frustration, pain, separation and illusion. Basically, it is through your body that you experience all the pain and suffering of your Being, and this occurs on the level of your Ego.

It is necessary that you understand the connection between your Ego and body, for you will then see how they interpret that information which is yours, that is, which flows from your higher dimensional Being.

I have stated in the Transmissions that your physical body is the consciousness of the Earth. And your consciousness, which is projected into the body, adds to the memory and growth of the Earth itself.

The Earth-body, to which you now project, consists of many frequencies, some being more dense than others. For instance, the tissues of the bones are heavier than brain tissue, and the same relationship exists between all other tissues within the body, but it is all one flow of energy. You have been educated into believing that everything you see and feel in the Third-dimension is separated. It is important to begin to understand that your Earth-body is a multi-density organism and as its parts are not separate from each other, the total body is not separate from all other Earth bodies, for it is one Earth.

The body and all its organs and tissues are connected in various patterns - the Morphogenetic Patterns. You heard in the last Transmission that your body patterns are replicas of the original patterns established in the Radiation Belts. These replicated patterns resonate continually through memory with the original Morphogenetic Patterns. You were told that these patterns are not quite the same as the original ones and are now not resonating in perfect harmony with the primal patterns.

128

Walk in the Light

The reason your present patterns are not resonating harmoniously with the original ones is that distortions have occurred. These distortions appear to your consciousness as disease, illness, pain and emotional and mental disturbances. In other words, if you feel disharmony of any kind, it tells you that your body is not resonating with its original morphogenesis.

To make this clearer I want you to picture in your mind a mold which is used for making jello. This mold will have cleavage and patterns which make it distinctive and will create indentations with the jello mixture as it sets. What you will notice is that every time you make jello it will always look the same. It will be the same size and pattern. In other words it always follows the original pattern. The finished product is harmonious with the mold in which it is made.

Suppose one day you drop the mold and accidentally stand on it. This will cause changes to its structure. You try and repair it but cannot get it back to its original state. After this, every time you make your jello in this mold it does not look quite the same as it did before. Its distortions are seen and its appearance is not harmonious with the original shape with which the mold was crafted.

This is similar to what has occurred with the Earth body, for it no longer replicates the original morphogenetic pattern. Imperfections have occurred and are now constantly replicated. Its memory of the original pattern is lost and all the new cells made by the body will replicate the deformed cells, and these cells are so distorted that they are referred to as being diseased cells, for they continue to mirror the deformities. What then is the answer to this?

Your medical scientists view these distorted patterns as being outside entities invading the body and virtually eating it up. Their treatment follows the Astral concept - seek and destroy. Such methods only tend to weaken the fabric of the organism and further destroy the harmony. There are those who consider that these distortions should be treated as Nature would treat them, whatever "Nature" is. They attempt to use vitamins, minerals and herbs which, they trust, will supply the energies and raw materials to heal or harmonise the patterns. Although these methods help, they do not address the problem of harmonizing the body with the original patterns. There are others who follow the "homeopathic" method and use simple substances to resonate and harmonize various structures of the body. It is impossible to use one simple substance to resonanate with the total patterns that represent the whole body and re-establish a return to the original pattern. Nevertheless these practitioners are achieving some success. However, because they expect individual plants and mineral substances to initiate a complete change in the total organism, they only just touch the outer perimeters of the body. Others practice the laying on of hands and mental healing. Every one of these has an effect on the functioning of the body, but none achieves total resonance, for the body is a conglomeration of various energies and unless the full spectrum of resonant frequencies are applied to alter the dissonant pattern, healing will not occur.

Although the body consists of a multitude of varying patterns of different densities and frequencies, there is one major hierarchial pattern, and it is this pattern which brings them all together as one unit. Another hierarchial pattern is one frequency which set into motion the creation of the Universe. This is viewed by many as the "Word of God" referred to in the Christian Bible.

We are not seeking a "Word", for Brahman does not speak. Your speech is of a Third-dimensional nature and only occurs on the Third-dimension. The Earth, its substance and consciousness is far removed from the center of Brahman, for it did not occur on the first or other outflows of Light. However, the key-note of the Earth is the one which responds to the morphogenetic pattern that constitutes its Nature.

Remember how I spoke of the seed in the last Transmission. All the patterns of becoming are contained in the seed and are released in the various stages of growth and maturity. The seed awaits its note to open; the warmth of the sun, the moisture of the earth, the energies contained in the soil, all constitute the music and growth. The human body has its memory patterns lodged in its DNA and these are fully activated in the sperm/ovum. The body then unfolds in a series of changes over decades and has the potential to last about 120 years. However this age is rarely attained due to the distortions continually occurring through the Ego's participation in the Illusion of the Astrals.

The body form which you see on the Third-dimension has its origins on the highest level of the Third-dimension. The upper radiation belt which surrounds the Earth contains within it all the original patterns which are replicated on the Earth. These energy belts consist of high frequency energies which have been termed "Etheric". The highest etheric frequencies found in the Third-dimension are those which emanate from the Sun. Being of such high frequency, they are moving at an extremely fast rate. The further these energies move away from the Sun the denser they become, or they slow down. Their slowest or most dense form is seen as being the matter or substance of the Earth.

The physical or Earth-body expresses "life" or consciousness due to the flow through it of your consciousness. The Ayon frequencies that emanate from the Sun act as a carrier of all the life energies as well as of your consciousness as they

131

move toward the Earth. Together with this is the progression of the Elemental consciousness which is responsible for maintaining the Morphogenetic Patterns throughout the Universe and all Dimensions. Here they hold together those energies that appear as your form.

For consciousness - your consciousness - to reach into the Third-dimensional experience, it must attach itself to various energy transformations which step down the frequencies of the energies which carry it. In many of the old writings existing in the memory of the planet, these step-down transformers have been referred to as "Chakras".

Chakras are energy vortices which have a two-way action. They step-up energies, allowing consciousness to move away from the Third-dimension into the Fourth-dimension and beyond. Built into the physical body are the endocrine glands which ground all Light and consciousness received into the Third-dimension. Information is then moved out into the Third-dimension by the five senses, which constitute a two-way switch for the reception of information experienced through interaction on the Third-dimension.

The endocrine glands work in harmony with the Etheric chakras which form an energy envelope around the body which is termed the Etheric Body. The etheric chakras are tuned to the Radiation Belts and constantly resonate with the Morphogenetic Patterns there. The Etheric System is not much different from the physical body, only it is not so dense. It too has a limited existence for it decays and breaks down not long after the death and decomposition of the physical body.

Beyond the etheric range of frequencies lie the Fourth-dimensional frequencies. The lower levels of the Fourth-dimension consist of frequencies which are more dense than those found in the higher levels of this dimension. It is the frequency of the Ego, and unfortunately the frequency where the Astral Lords work. Also it is the realm of the Illusion.

The Ego, too, replicates the chakra system that is found in the Etheric Body, except that it has three additional chakra centers found above the Crown Center. These Fourth-dimensional chakras connect the Ego to the etheric consciousness as well as to the frequencies of the higher levels of the Fourth-dimension, which in turn harmonise with all other levels of Brahman.

Your Earth experience exists in consciousness where the higher frequencies flow through the Ego's chakras to the Earth-body. Although in this Solar System your consciousness flows through the Sun to your Ego and Earth-body, not every Ego has as yet a higher Fourth-dimensional body. It is through many experiences on the Third-dimension that one forms this higher dimensional form of consciousness, and the majority of beings projecting into the Egos on the Fourth-dimension have not previously centered their consciousness actively in that dimension. In the initial stages of development, consciousness is grounded in the understanding of the Third-dimension for the moving of information to the Ego. Once the frequencies of this dimension are expanded and understood, the Ego is able to move consciousness to the higher dimensions where there is the foundation of the Light Body, or Fourth-dimensional body, which grows also in Light as it begins to expand its frequencies back into the Fifth-dimension and so on.

You have already been told that your consciousness moves from the higher dimensional Stars in this Galaxy through the Sun of its Solar System. This consciousness is what is best termed the "raw material" of consciousness which will grow and expand in Light as it moves through its Earth Experience.

The chakra system is the means whereby you are connected to all that you are. There are seven major chakras in the Etheric and Ego systems. These are called Base, Sacral, Solar Plexus, Heart, Throat, Brow and Crown. These are responsible for moving the bulk of information through all the bodies. In addition to these major chakras are several other chakras which are responsible for moving energies and information received from the five senses. These chakras are also found in the Etheric and Ego bodies. Their corresponding centres are found in the physical body at the following points: Spleen, Stomach, Liver, Thymus, Left Gonad, Right Gonad, Left Knee, Right Knee, Left Sole, Right Sole, Left Breast, Right Breast, Junction of the Clavicles, Left Palm, Right Palm, Left Eye, Right Eye. In addition to these there are many Transformer glands which move energies to and from the organs in the body,

As the body unfolds in the womb of the mother, so too is the Etheric body formed, for the Etheric Body is also a Third-dimensional frequency. The Ego and Etheric bodies move through the Radiation Belts toward the Earth-body and pass through the Life Vortex which forms close to where the birth is to occur. As the fetus moves through the birth canal, the higher bodies move through the Life Vortex, and at the time of birth all unite as one unit in expressing Light on the Third-dimension. Now you begin your Walk in Light.

Not all is perfect as the walk of life begins. The molds for the Morphogenetic patterns have been distorted over many generations. Not only are the body patterns altered, but also that pattern with which the Ego should resonate. So where does that leave you in your desire for One Light?

*

Walk in the Light

At the beginning of this Transmission I referred to three major energy frequencies which are constantly moving from the higher dimensions into the Third-dimension. These frequencies of your Being are "feelings", and they are experienced on this dimension as Love, Freedom, and Success. As they move through the distorted patterns of your Ego, the distortions promote confusion and suffering in your consciousness at the Ego level, and pain and frustration at the level of the body.

For the higher frequencies to reach your Third-dimensional consciousness, you need to have developed higher vehicles of expression on the Fourth-dimension. It may take one or two lives on Earth to develop such a body, or it may take several more depending on the intensity of the Life Experience. For instance, a life lived through wars, where the Ego is confronted with personal pain and suffering and shares in the sufferings of others, will create an expansion of the higher frequencies in the Ego as the higher feelings are given expression. For, during episodes of intense pain and deprivation, the Ego often learns to discard karma by becoming less self-centered. This sort of experience will quicken the formation of the higher Fourth-dimensional Light Body. Many other life experiences will also generate a movement toward higher frequencies of Brahman.

At present there are many millions of individual Egos who have developed a Fourth-dimensional Light Body but are totally unaware of it, which was the case with you, Jon. That is why throughout the Transmissions, I have encouraged you to remember, and keep on remembering, for you could fall asleep to it once more. That body is of pure Light and it is now YOU. In your quiet moments you will "feel" its presence and know that it is you.

In this moment of consciousness there are many people

Enter the Vortex as One Light

who are reaching out in their feelings, attempting to find and experience their Light Body or, as they term it, their "Soul". The Illusion has become the barrier which separates them from achieving their desires. Still working in the Illusion, they seek God, for they are told that this God is their personal salvation. They are unaware that this God is their Own Being - their "Soul" or Light Body. Many others attach their need for contact with their inner Light to people of the past, such as Jesus, Buddha or any other "luminary" who pronounces that they are the Saviors of Mankind. Giving your Light other names and to others only deepens your separation. Your Light, and only YOUR LIGHT will lead YOU from the Illusion of the Third-dimension.

Some of you have walked the Earth for many lives and have developed Light expression on the Fifth and higher dimensions, and still you are unaware. The Astral Lords have "consciousness washed" your Ego into believing that you do not possess a higher body of Light, and that is where the God concept originated. That God concept is far removed from the creative essence of Brahman ,which is ALL Light.

Also there are many walking the Earth now who are not focused on the Astral Illusion, and they are awaiting some sign or some Being which will unlock their feeling of separation and fulfil their yearning for Freedom. They will find that The Vortex of Light and Healing is the key that will flood the Earth with Light and Healing. This will be true Freedom.

How does your Light Being convey information to you such as freedom, love and success? It does not talk in words, for words and their thought patterns only come into existence as your brain becomes aware of the frequencies flowing through it at a rate that it can translate and create coherent thought patterns, which are the basis of Third-dimensional consciousness.

The Ego stores the patterns of thought which the brain translates into awareness. It is obvious that it is the Ego which receives the higher frequencies first.

How does a frequency such as Freedom move through the Ego, and why is it called Freedom? To answer that I will start with its expression on the Third-dimension. There is a constant inner urge moving through consciousness to be free. But free from what? It is at this level that all confusion about the frequency begins.

As the Light flow of the Freedom frequency moves through your Ego, it becomes tainted, bent or dented, for the mold of the Ego is changed from its original morphogenetic pattern. It no longer resonates with its original signature, since it now replicates many of the Astral patterns, and conveys these to the Body Consciousness, which in turn distorts the morphogenetic pattern of the body. Both the Ego and Body no longer resonate in complete harmony with the higher dimensional Light Bodies, so all the frequencies flowing from the Light sources become distorted in their manifestation on the Third-dimension.

The Freedom Frequency continually flows from the heart of Brahman through all dimensions. Now, because of the bad reception of the Ego, it manifests on this dimension, causing feelings of restriction and uneasiness.

At the lowest level of expression you see it as a need for a change, possibly a change in location. Such a change is felt as being free - free to move to other parts of the Earth. It is never seen as complete freedom even on this level, due to the construction of borders and restricted access to different communities.

Again, freedom is sought by changing employment, or becoming involved in owning one's own business. This does not lead to freedom, due to the restrictions on all activity imposed by governments and their bureaucrats.

Many see the creation of wealth as leading to freedom. However, wealth creation only leads to being captive to the drive to make more money and this again does not lead to any further freedom.

Others turn to Churches and religious cults, who have, so they say, the ability to free their adherents' souls. But they must wait for the After-life to gain such freedom, for God put them on Earth to suffer, as that is the only way that God will love them.

Freedom is the flow of joy, love and success. These frequencies of feeling all exist as one emanation of Brahman and are not single, isolated energies. Isolation of feeling only exists at the Ego frequency, where its energies are separated into streams of consciousness on the Fourth and Third dimensions. When the Ego lens is discolored, the expression of the pure, undifferentiated energy becomes altered and confused.

It may seem unusual to state that the Success Frequency is a flow from the higher dimension. Most will agree that Love is a flow from Brahman, but the Success Frequency is not comprehended because it is received in a much more distorted flow from One Light than any other frequency.

Success is often viewed as being highly Astral and, no doubt, the Astrals use that frequency to their advantage, for it forms a corner-stone of their Illusion.

When you look around your Earth dimension how many people do you see who are truly experiencing their own "success"? Success is based on the personal need for accomplishment, which is based on achieving those goals which are Illusion oriented. Success is commonly understood here as being the need to accomplish goals, for the marketing of suc-

138

cess is based on achieving many goals that are set by the Ego and its relationship with the Illusion. Unfortunately every goal accomplished is supplanted by the need to create another goal, for no successful goals ever provide the sense of true success, for they never lead to Being. The frequencies of your Being are "feelings", and the success frequency is also a feeling. Feeling always exists on all dimensions even if it comes through distorted by your Ego.

Actually, success is an expression of the "I" - the One Light, that lifts the consciousness to higher expressions of Brahman. Success builds higher frequencies and expanded dimensions of Light, for it opens your consciousness to experience all the Universes of Brahman. When the success frequency is blocked and restricted, pain is experienced by the body and there is suffering to the Ego, and, in fact, much illness results from the inability to allow success to flow. The Ego uses illness to blame the Body, and Inner talking follows. "It's your fault, your weakness," berates the Ego. "How do you expect me to reflect One Light? You are the failure, not I!"

The failure frequency emanates from the Astral domain, and not from Brahman. This blocking or failure frequency is molded from what is commonly described as "attitude". You all display attitudes, but for most of the time you are unaware of them. You say, "I have not got an attitude." That is because its root cause is now lost to your consciousness.

There are no good attitudes, although you often say there are. All attitudes are of a negative source. When you refer to someone having a positive attitude to something, you consider the attitude to be positive because it falls in line with the purpose of the Astral Illusion.

You will remember, Jon, that you displayed an attitude reflecting a low self image when you first learned that you had to move the Transmissions out to the World; you even attempted to encourage Rose to take on the task. It is not uncommon for people to have attitudes similar to this. You may also remember, Jon, when you were young, that your older brother always pleased your parents. He seemed to do everything perfectly well, or so you thought. Many of your efforts were passed by, or you were never encouraged by your parents in your efforts to please. You first developed a sense of insecurity, and this, over several years, began to harden or crystallize. Crystallization is the formation of an attitude. Once the attitude is formed, you no longer even think the feeling but react automatically to a situation. It is common for many people caught in their attitudes and reactions to say, "There's nothing I can do about it. That's the way I'm made. You can't change that. Everybody is different." These are the words of an individual who is so tied up in attitudes that he or she has lost all sense of personal direction and is constantly reacting in the Astral Illusion.

Even when you are successful later in life, and everyone tells you so time and time again, your happiness and self esteem do not stay high, for unconsciously your attitude prompts you into feeling insecure, and you do not know why.

BUT NOW YOU DO!

Attitudes do not only exist in individuals, but they are reflected in group action. A number of individuals may band together to start a new profession, or a new religion. Constantly they are threatened by the establishment and they develop patterns to strengthen their position. They are always on the defensive and in attacking mode. They develop an attitude to react whenever anyone says something that they see as being destructive to their cause. After many years they grow and become accepted by the establishment, however the attitude remains

Walk in the Light

and even at their time of acceptance they still react aggressively to situations which would no longer damage their image. So you see that individuals often take on the group attitude and when new people join the group they are unconsciously drawn into expressing that attitude. All attitudes are based on the Astral frequency of FEAR, and fear moves consciousness away from the Light.

Differing from insecurity, false modesty, or the disguising of one's true conceit, is another expression of Astral attitude based on fear. In most instances false modesty is used to gain an advantage from some unsuspecting individual. It is used by the Ego to increase its power over others in the Illusion.

Your need to be successful is an expression of your Light. If you do not honestly acknowledge your success you are not acknowledging your expression.

Of course you need to recognize that you have a particular attitude. Don't worry about trying to find your attitudes, for others will quickly tell you. If not verbally, then by their reaction to you every time you express them. They may just turn off, or they may attack you, expressing some attitude of their own. At these times you probably blame others for their reactions to your attitude, and say in turn that they have an attitude when in fact they may not. That is your weakness. Once you see your attitude you need not continually and remorsefully go back to your childhood or teenage years in order to objectify it, for that will lead you back into despair. What you must do is acknowledge that you Walk in Light!

The magnificent healing force which flows out of the heart of Brahman is the expression of the frequency of "Love". Everyone expects to be loved, for love manifests throughout all frequencies in all dimensions. The Astral Lords, and their Entities attempt to limit Love to being a human experience, for

141

as they have turned their faces away from the pure Light of Brahman, they negate the essence of the frequency of Love.

Love is the Healing frequency; it is the energy of the Vortex, the healing force of all things. It is only through love that any return to wholeness is attained. Love, then, is the unifying energy of Brahman, and is expressed on the Third-dimension as unconditional "love", and this is the highest frequency which it manifests on this dimension. This unconditionality is its expression on all other dimensions too, for Brahman is unconditional in Its expression of Love in Its creation.

Do not keep bullying your Ego into letting go of its Illusion. You feel that in order to have Light flow into your body you must constantly fight your Ego. That is not necessary. Your Light IS manifesting here on the Earth. However you are constantly believing that you must change or cleanse your Ego in an aggressive manner. You could forget about your Ego and just Be!

To explain further, your Light is flowing from your Fourth-dimensional being constantly through your Ego and into your body and out into the world through your five senses. Its flow is distorted by the Ego and Body and everyone out there in the Illusion. However your Light IS HERE NOW, distorted or not. All you need to do is KNOW this and FEEL it. Once you feel it, it is still the same Light.

Meditation is an atunement with your higher being. It is your higher being communicating with itself. When you meditate you need not perform visualizations of any kind, all you need to do is feel your Love, Freedom and Success, and move on the crystal strands of your Light to your Being in the higher dimensions. Bypass the Ego, and move in your Light. Then you will then see a transformation occur naturally to your Ego as it is pulled away from the Illusion.

Walk in the Light

What you will then see is that the Earth is filled with Light and that you constantly Walk in the Light.

You strive to be and see the Light, when already you are the Light. How many times have I expressed this in these Transmissions? Now you are being moved deeper into the Vortex.

Have you ever considered why the Astral Lords do not deny the need for you to seek your Light? Because they know that you will never find it as long as you continually seek it through their Illusion. They say that you must suppress all desires in order to be "free", however suppression actually denies you the freedom that you seek. You are told that you must fight your Ego, which they claim is in league with the devil. How true. The "devil" is a concept of the Illusion, and if you are to fight the "devil", you must fight the Illusion. This becomes an impossible task. The next block to accomplishment is that you are exhorted to seek "perfection", and as the Illusion is imperfect, this too becomes an impossibility. You give up, fail and fall back into the comfort of the Illusion. This is the line of least resistance.

Your Light is flowing constantly through your Ego and to the Earth. It has no purpose or direction, and loses its impact on the consciousness of the Earth, but it is still there. You do not need to seek it in the manner which you have been following for many years, but you do need to acknowledge it. You walk in the Light and you see it not. All you need to do is have eyes to see, for you are blinded to the Light by your attitude toward it. Cast off that attitude, and allow your Love, Freedom and Success to shine through you as you be the Light, and your Ego has no other choice than to follow you, and you will Walk in the Light on all Dimensions forever.

Transmission
Twelve

The Healing Light

Y ou are a healing being, for it is the essence of your Nature that moves you to create Light and Healing within the Third-dimension.

As you look out of your body through its five senses you begin to conceptualise that the dimension consists of a duality of energies. This is reinforced as you perceive that the body you are extending your consciousness from is separate from what it perceives. This creates a sense of confusion which moves your consciousness away from oneness.

The Third-dimensional Universe has its form due to two major energies. Your scientists have labelled similar energies as protons and electrons, and the difference between these two energies is due to what is termed polarities. These two polarities are actually one energy, having distinct frequencies due to their rotational movement. One moves in what is best described as a clockwise movement, whilst the other moves in a counter clockwise motion, and it is this which creates the frequency of polarity or opposites. The Earth moves in an opposite spin motion to the Sun, and the same principle applies to all matter of the Third-dimensional Universe. The use of terms "positive" and "negative" to express polarity is not fitting. I have called the energy polarity of the Earth - Kayon energy, and that of the Sun - Ayon energy.

The basic matter of the Universe, and in particular the Earth, is formed by Kayon energy which has high magnetic fields. The Sun is composed mainly of Ayon energy, having high electrical fields.

The Earth-body is composed largely of Kayon energy, and its form and composition are held together by the Etheric field which surrounds it and is composed of Ayon energy.

The Earth-body, being mainly Kayon energy, uses its magnetic fields to understand and interpret its environment, and these magnetic sensors are called "the five senses". It is necessary that the information about the Third-dimension be conveyed to the Fourth-dimension, and the interconnection between the senses and the chakra vortices of the Etheric or electrical body are used for this purpose.

As the Ayon energy moves from the Sun to the Earth, it carries with it the consciousness from the higher dimensions to the Earth, and it allows you to move your consciousness through the Earth-body and use its sensors to understand and experience this environment.

Instability in these energies is experienced when the resonance between the Earth and Etheric bodies occurs. The information flow is distorted and imbalance to the energies occurs. This is what is called illness or disharmony.

Keeping in mind that the Earth is also a living organism composed mainly of Kayon frequencies, and that if its resonance with the Ayon frequencies from the Sun is disturbed, it too will suffer imbalance and disharmony. And this has occurred by Mankind's participation in the Illusion.

The beginning of all disease and disharmony began when the Astral Lords moved their illusionary web over the consciousness of all Egos manifesting their Light on the Earth dimension.

You must not think that this Astral Illusion is something new, and that formerly isolated races such as the Australian Aborigine and those of the North American Indians and the races on the South American and African continents were free of the forces of the Illusion. These races were never as isolated as the regular history books would have you believe. History is politically motivated and is changed at will to suit the needs of the ruling class of a place. After two generations, the new history becomes factual in the minds of the populace of the time. True history lies in the memory patterns of the cells of the Earth and its bodies, as well as in the memory banks of the Radiation belt.

The Illusion existed well before Atlantis, and existed in the consciousness of all peoples from when your Ego first projected to this dimension. There are many Egos currently moving through this Earth experience who are beginning to feel stress as they move in and out of the Illusion. It is healing that will complete their ascension to One Light.

So it is "healing " which must be acknowledged by you, for it forms an integral part of the Vortex. Healing begins with the individual.

I would have you consider briefly what the word "humanitarian" means to you. Is it extending selfless help to an individual or to many who are suffering the indignities of a harsh life in a particular country or place? Is it not true that a humanitarian does not seek rewards for his or her work? The only reward being the love given back from those whom they have helped. Many so-called humanitarians usually receive accolades from others in office. They are awarded prizes and become famous in the eyes of the World. This ends in an Ego trip for some. Often the fame and glory will outweigh the purpose underlying the humanitarian act, and this new celebrity becomes a useful tool in promoting the hidden agendas of the Astral Entities in their quest for wealth and power.

The Christ spirit moved through the Ethers of the Third-dimension some two thousand years ago. The message continually repeated was that each of you should learn to love the other as did the Christ. This is the underlying purpose of all humanitarian work.

Sit quietly now and consider how Christ loved humankind. In no way does it mirror the Astral version. The Christ Light moved through the Ego called Jesus, and Jesus mirrored the Christ in the Third-dimension. The Astral version has it that Jesus died on a cross in reparation for the sins of Mankind. There is no doubt that the Astrals opposed the Christ Light, for it would turn all human Egos away from their Illusion. The only way they could counteract the flow of Light was to create altered concepts around the event, by introducing changes to their advantage and by hood-winking the consciousness of the Egos through these changes.

Through their entities they formed a "Church", which was designed to take charge of all aspects of the Christ teachings. The "Church" of the Entities then became the authority and the only way by which an individual could receive the message. Only by following its doctrines could one be saved to the Light. The entities altered much of the writings of the early followers, and made sure that the work of each of the four scribes did not vary in content. It was important that the man Jesus was seen as the Christ, and could be raised to the status of a God. Now that they had created a God they could draw great energy for the Astral Lords from these believers.

To all this they added the Armageddon event, which has been used to hold the population of the churches in constant fear of a terrible end for all Mankind.

After seeing how much control they could achieve over so many million souls, they used the same formula with all other religions in the world, for all faiths on the Earth wallow in fear of what their gods can do to them should they stray from the path. Later they moved the same principles into creating control over the Crusades by forming mystical organizations to oversee and continue the wars in the name of freedom, and to further their hold over the minds and consciousness of humanity. They even used these clandestine organizations to create wars and revolutions to keep control of the governmental structures of the Nations.

These "Churches" of the Astrals are not concerned with assisting individuals to reach personal power and freedom, for this will only take power from themselves, and they know that they would be helpless to prevent a mass change in consciousness. However such a mass change will occur regardless of their plots and subterfuge, for they cannot imprison the Light of all individuals.

How did the Christ love Mankind? Unconditionally! He did not die for your sins as you have been often told! If that were so then there would be no sinners now, some two thousand years later. The Entities responsible for the Church creation found it profitable to have their followers believe that their sins have been forgiven, for they knew that these believers would happily fall back asleep in the Illusion and under their control.

The Healing Light

These Transmissions are moving your consciousness into the Vortex where the healing of your Ego is occurring, for all healing moves from the center of Brahman. Brahman is Love, and Love is healing. The love of the Christ created waves of healing which passed through the Earth, and still do. The love of the Christ is healing, and you must heal yourself and the Earth as you emanate the love of the Christ.

In explaining the moving of healing forces I will describe a personal situation such as you may have experienced. When a loved one of yours is ill and suffering, whether it is another human or an animal, your love moves out to them, you feel compassion, your mind becomes troubled, and you enter into a state of fear. You feel helpless and inadequate as you see the life force draining away. All the great authorities and their medical science has been of no avail, in fact they only seemed to have made the condition worse. You feel an inner urge to touch and extend your love. You cry out in yourself for help. You pray. You seek advice from others - faith healers, in fact anyone. Yet there is no change.

What do you fear? You do not fear the pain and suffering of the loved one. You fear a personal loss, a loss of companionship, and being left alone in the world.

Do you consider how the loved one feels? You speak with them, and all you ask is how they feel. What you really mean is how much pain are they in, and do they feel any better than the previous day?

However it is important for the one who suffers to truly enter into their feelings about their illness. They must come to a realization of their feeling about their present state of consciousness in their suffering. They must attempt to know in themselves why they are ill, for they do know. Once they express their true feelings they either recover or die peacefully.

And their feelings about their illness will be totally different from yours.

You are moved to help, for the love within you has no other direction. Love does heal all, but why has not your love healed your loved one? How did the Christ spirit heal man? Within the purity of the being of the Christ Spirit was mirrored the cause of the illness back to the one suffering, and they wanted to be healed of their transgressions. Were they not told, "Go and sin no more!"? Meaning that, if they were to continue to remain whole, then they should not follow their previous life path.

During your periods of illness and suffering it is only by becoming closer to your own Light that you will mirror the cause of your suffering. Your attitudes and your karma of illness must be felt by your Ego in its consciousness for any healing to occur. Healing is reflecting and mirroring that which you truly are.

There is little difference between an old worn out body - one that has passed its use by date and has expired- and one that is controlled by a tormented Ego which rejects Light to its body. One is actually dead and the other might as well be.

A recognition of what and who you are, and why you are, is the font of all healing, for until you begin to acknowledge what you are and why you behave in a particular manner, you will continue to suffer the illness of the Third-dimensional Illusion.

Often the concern you experience when you witness the suffering of others is only the reflection of the fear which exists in you, and unconsciously you wonder when your turn will come. You cannot heal another until you become whole. It is not the healing of the body that is your prime concern, rather it is the condition of your own Ego that matters, for while you continue to exhibit behaviors of attitude and think negatively about others, you limit the healing in you.

Begin by loving yourself, not the false Ego self, but the beautiful Light you truly are. Perhaps you find it difficult to love that Light which you are, not knowing quite how to recognize It as yet. However It is there, and once you begin to move your consciousness towards that inner something, and away from the Ego and the Illusion, you will begin to feel the flow of love within you.

Constantly think toward your being. Think directionally if that helps. Feel inwardly for it; feel outwardly, around you, or above you, but feel for your Light, ask for it to reveal itself to you. Your inner Essence is waiting for you NOW.

Think of yourself as being burdened down by excessive layers of clothes which are heavy and hot. These layers represent all the karma that you have acquired over many life experiences on the Earth. They are continually demanding some recognition from your Ego. They have never satisfied their desire for fame and greatness, and they demand fulfilment. They are the desperate desires of your Ego over many thousands of years, still wanting the fame and power that the Illusion offers. Take time to observe how these influence your reaction when you are placed in a demanding situation. Work to peel them back and lighten your load. As you do this you will open your eyes to the Illusion, and as you atone, you will move your consciousness in harmony with that glowing flow of Light within you. Listen for its voice, await its Name, for it is your real name, and then you will call it down into this body of yours and the Third-dimension, for you will become One Light.

Your initial daily contact will give you stability and pull you free from all Illusion, lessening the stress that has been building up in your mind and body.

Enter the Vortex as One Light

You cannot love others until you begin to love yourself, and you will not love yourself until you become what you truly are. As you take one step closer to your inner being it will move two steps closer to you. You will feel a quickening in your consciousness. Do not allow your Ego to move between you, for it will only sow doubt. Move in trust to the inflow of Light.

Gradually you will begin to allow the healing to flow, for you only need to let it happen; you cannot decide that healing should be. Once true healing flows through you, without your attempting to control or direct it, you will heal the loved one. Your Ego considers that it has the power to direct healing when and where it wants to. However you have now passed beyond the Ego's demands, for it must now resonate in harmony with the Light Essence which is you.

"One Light" is moving through the consciousness on the Earth and drawing many into the Vortex of Light and Healing. I am aware of much of the hardness imbedded in the consciousness of Mankind, however the penetration of the Light consciousness into the mass of people depends upon how quickly you move yourself into the Vortex. To do so you must take these Transmissions into your consciousness and live them daily. The greater the number who open the Light into the dimension, the greater will be the power of Love moving to others.

Light has constantly been flowing to the Earth since your consciousness penetrated this dimension. However it has become directionless. Some has been chanelled through the Illusion to the Astral Lords. This has been freely given by you in your religious beliefs. Other Light is scattered without purpose throughout the ethers. Once you become One Light you will perceive Light everywhere on the Earth.

Once you become aligned with your Light Body, you

will constantly be that Light Body on the Third-dimension through the Earth-body, and, through the power of your Being, you will resonate with all the other Light dispersed across the planet. This will give it direction and healing for the Earth, and the Earth will begin to move its ascent into the Fourth-dimension.

You, like me, exist on all dimensions. I am harmonizing the Light on the Earth, and all others who open through these Transmissions will widen the Vortex and consciously free the Earth.

Will you join me? You can, all you need is to want to, to seek your self and be One in All - Cry out for Light!

Transmission
Thirteen

Interdimensional Being

In the last Transmission I referred to the various layers of
your past life experiences that seem to cloak or surround
your Ego, distorting the direction of the Light flow through
your Ego as it moves into the Third-dimension. That Light is
your higher consciousness, and it is that Light which the Earth
awaits to hasten its ascension into the Fourth-dimension.

How often do you fall back into old habits by repeating
or living out old Ego life experiences and desires? Have you
noticed how uncomfortable you now feel once you allow these
negative frequencies to express themselves through your Ego
and body! Don't you feel helpless as this darkness once more
descends over your Third-dimension expression? You now
know that you cannot lose your contact with your inner Light,
but you find it difficult to command these old frequencies to
depart again.

Interdimensional Being

Initially, Jon, you again resorted to self blame until you realized that these dark frequencies were none other than Razparil demanding power and recognition, enticing your Ego to serve him, with the reward of power and Astral control. What you must know is that Razparil and those of his ilk cannot survive without Ego contact. Left to his own devices he will eventually become an empty shell devoid of all energy.

He is still like an old suit of clothing to your Ego, one that is well worn and fits comfortably, however it has now passed its use by date. Without a captive Ego, he is no longer a force on the Astral dimension, so he returns, watches and waits for your lapses into old habits, lapses which will soon become a rarity to your Ego.

These lapses often appear as old desires, those which still consider that they should be fulfilled, for the Illusion is rampant with desire for power and greatness. Your Ego is much like the Earth-body to which it is attached. As your Ego is the focus point for the flow of the higher energies, the body is the focus point for the expression of the Earth's consciousness in the Third-dimension. They are both passive frequencies which act out the manifestation of the Light or darkness which flows through them.

It is timely that you place these two frequencies in correct perspective, for they are not something that you should hate or detest. You must not consider that you must subdue or sublimate them, or bring them under the control of your will. Those forces which you are constantly applying to the Ego for control and domination are none other than the desires you have built up over the eons of life experiences on this dimension. The Ego mirrors those desires into the consciousness and memories of the body, which in turn mirrors them into the Third-dimension, affecting all others with whom contact is made.

155

Enter the Vortex as One Light

As you experience these reactions within your consciousness you become confused. You believe that such actions stem from some innate consciousness of the Ego, and often they are seen as a reflection of your higher being. The Ego cunningly pretends that it is the body and not itself, which is causing all the disruptions, and it feels that the body should be punished for such behavior. This is a common fault which occurs throughout the consciousness of Mankind, where the Ego's deceptions are labelled as Truth, and are but a subterfuge of the Astrals in the distortion of the Illusion.

Remember, Jon, when Razparil smothered your Ego in darkness and you called out for Light and awakened Sizzond? Sizzond was not imprisoned in darkness but was "asleep" to your Ego. During your desperate struggle with the forces of the Illusion it was Sizzond whose Light exposed the Illusion for what it really is.

From then onward you gained strength and confidence which enabled you to write about the Transmissions and how they were destined for Mankind. You must realize now that your Ego is not your enemy, and that it too is not imprisoned in the Illusion, but only requires freedom from its old desires. It must now remain focused on the Light which flows through it, for if it submits once more to the old desires and demands, it will move power back to the Astral Lords.

The constant flow of One Light through your Ego will give power to the body frequency and in turn this will burn off the garbage which has attached itself to your Ego. For if nothing remains for it to attach to, then the Ego is free for eternity to move the Light of Brahman to the Earth.

You will remember that during the Transmissions you recorded for "One Light", you were told that the Ego was created as a frequency which was seen as the servant of the Higher

Light Body. How then can something which was created as a perfect frequency not act in its perfect manner? In your consciousness you must know and feel that your Ego is perfect and does not work against the love and feeling that flows through it. What has occured is that, during its long experience in the Astral Illusion, it has also suffered distortion to its morphogenetic patterns. These alterations have been expressed by the desires of the Astral Illusion which have impregnated its body or form. These are such that they are of a frequency which causes it to act "automatically" in harmony with the frequencies of the Illusion.

When, initially, I spoke of the early contact of the Egos with the Astral Illusion, I related how, at first, the Ego tended to vacillate between the desires of the Illusion and the flow of Light from your interdimensional being. The longer the Ego was exposed to the Astral Illusion through many life experiences, the more dense became the illusionary coat which eventually committed the Ego to the Astral Illusion.

Now that your awareness is increasing and you feel daily the flow of Light into your body's consciousness, you will no more require further life experience on the Third-dimension, for once the body is exposed to the Light flow completely, it too is whole, and the Earth is also whole on that segment of its consciousness. You only have to do it once, but that once must be complete. The inflowing Light will burn up all the dross that clings to your Ego. Then, when it is directed to your Earth-body, it will act in a similar manner and re-establish the morphogenetic frequencies which will free the Earth-body of all distortion and illusionary desires.

These Transmissions you are now recording have to a large extent concentrated on healing, for the body and the Ego. If the body, through the Ego, reflects disharmony, which is a

157

corner stone of the Illusion, then it means that much of the Earth's consciousness is enmeshed in the Astral Illusion.

Once you begin to burn off the layers of desire which have been attracted to your Ego, and it reflects the pure Light of your Being, all the so-called illness of the body will cease to manifest. Now something beautiful occurs. These layers of illusionary desire seem to act like a cocoon, with the Ego being the chrysalis. Once the Ego breaks free from its cocoon it becomes the beautiful butterfly, which is free to express the Light and Love of Brahman.

Everything that is, is of Brahman, and is beautiful and pure in its frequency. There is no need to fight and blame your Ego, for it is only an Illusion which holds it captive. As you heal your Ego of its attachment to the Illusion, you are helping to restore the body to that frequency which is a release from the Illusion on the Third-dimension. With this freeing comes the awareness that you still have a responsibility to maintain the harmony of the body. You need to eat correctly, drink pure water and exercise regularly.

Keep well away from competitive sports, as, due to the attitudes involved with competitiveness, they are Astrally motivated and controlled. They tend to lead the Ego back into selfishness and greed. The Ego becomes motivated with false desire and the need for wealth, fame and approbation. The intensive training programmes are detrimental to the health of the body, causing undue stress and energy loss. A healthy body is one which becomes enlivened by non-stress exercise.

As you free the body of excessive stress, which is produced by participating in the Illusion, you will also free the Earth from the Illusion which is holding it back from its movement in consciousness.

The Earth, with its plants and animals, and the homes

constructed by many different animals, are not part of the Astral Illusion. It is only how one uses the products of the Earth, and for what purpose, which constitutes participation in the Illusion. If your Ego imposes its needs for its benefit, and to the destruction of the Earth, then it is entrenched in the Illusion.

It is the continual flow of Light passing through your Ego which allows the Earth-body to express its consciousness in an intelligent and inventive manner, which in turn enhances the growing consciousness of the Earth.

Through a sharing of consciousness by the Egos, individuals have developed specific skills that have become part of the growing consciousness and memory of the Earth and its body. These skills embrace all expressions of human consciousness and are seen in trades, professions, and arts, becoming more perfected by individual Egos as they move through many life experiences over many thousands of years.

Unfortunately all these developments are also taken into the Illusion, and are used by the Astral Lords in their disruption of the Earth's frequency. Most inventions that are drawn forth in consciousness are, in their initial pattern, used for the beneficial needs of Mankind. However, when these are taken into the Astral Illusion, they are used for destructive purposes.

You will now work with your Ego in directing Light to the Earth-body, and you will do this in a conscious manner, not as you have done before.

I am reminded again of your people, Rose, and how it took a long period of Earth time for them to become entrenched fully in the Illusion. They remained connected to the Earth and expressing their higher consciousness through their bodies. Their music and dance remained pure and helped direct their consciousness to their Light source and the Earth. Over many thousands of years they, too, added layers of Astrality to their

Egos. However, it was only when they embraced the culture of the Western World and its dependence on the Illusion, that they also cloaked their Egos with the denser layers of the Illusion. However, the peace and closeness to the Earth has stopped your people from being fully committed to the Illusion, for the Earth still speaks to you. You remembered much of what you were taught in your childhood, and after you embraced the original Transmissions you soared in consciousness as the Eagle and united your being with Zarine. The Vortex will open the Light Gate for many, as they too embrace these Transmissions, and they too will be free from all Illusion.

As your Ego becomes pure once more on the Fourth-dimension, it will channel Light to the Earth-body. You will still be You in the body, just as you are now, but you will FEEL different, for you will be the Light and Love of your higher dimensional being. You will retain all your memories and skills, for you could not exist on this planet without them.

What will change is how you express your Light into the Earth-dimension. There will be no greed, no anger, no pride, only an expression of the Love of Brahman. It is the purpose that underlies your actions that will change. You will have no destructive thoughts, feelings or actions, for these do not exist in Brahman.

You will be renewed in the Light of your consciousness, for now you will be expressing Me, and Zarine, through your bodies. You are no longer Jon and Rose, but Zadore and Zarine. You no longer need the names of the Illusion, for you are not that anymore. All others who move through the Vortex and burn off their illusionary desires will also become their real selves as One Light, expressing their true identity.

Move further into the Vortex as One Light.

Transmission
Fourteen

Earth Consciousness

A Transmission from the Earth:

Have you, after reading the Transmissions from the Sun and the Earth which were transcribed in "One Light", questioned the validity of these Transmissions? Some reasoned that these Transmissions were but a collection of holographically produced images and words communicated by Zadore which did not truly involve me. Why do so many people consider that consciousness and Light flow only through them and that human beings are the only organisms in the Universe to hold this position in Light?

After many thousands of years, during which you have committed your Ego consciousness to the concepts of the Astral Illusion, can you not envisage any other consciousness existing outside the Illusion? These Transmissions are given to you to break down those barriers which enslave your consciousness, and produce a myopic vision of consciousness which blinds you to all else in Brahman.

The greatest problem which you experience in the illusionary aspect of your consciousness is the attachment to your body. Intellectually you have reasoned and accepted that you are not your body. However you have not yet experienced this condition in the feeling aspect of your Ego, and at times of stress you revert to old habits.

Nor have you expressed true love for this body. Most of your "love" is only expressed in an Astral way. Your "love" is experienced sensually, where the form and shape express pleasure and admiration. When you find the form unbalanced, misshapened and overweight, it becomes an object of disdain. You work to retain its symmetery by exercise and diet not out of love for its needs and purposes, but for it to be accepted and admired by others. And you are driven into healing a sick body because you fear its loss, as you live in the Astral belief that the body is your creation and means of expression.

Should your intention be to restore your body's shape or health because you want your Light and Love to flow through it, and also that you recognize that your body is the Earth's body, then you are truly loving the body, unconditionally. Until you begin to love your body unconditionally, you cannot love Me.

When you express awe and love at the grandeur of my form, you are mirroring the beauty of how your body relates to the totality of my being.

When you love the Earth, you also love your body. Once you begin to feel and practice this you will cease your destructive efforts totally, for to harm my environment is to harm your own body.

Earth Consciousness

Mankind always names everything it becomes aware of. It called me the Earth, and many other names, however none of them actually apply to me, for I am a specific frequency in the Galaxy. Everything in the Universe is a frequency of the love of Brahman, for nothing is separate in Brahman. That is why I questioned why you would feel that the Earth, and for that matter, all the Stars and Planets in the Universe, would have no consciousness or Light. Only some of you believe that the dolphins, for example, have equal spiritual consciousness with human beings. Not until you move out of the Astral Illusion and clear your Ego of misconceptions about the sole importance of Mankind, will you be able to be one with all consciousness, and recognize it. For I am a living Being expressing my Light and consciousness to other dimensions beyond this Third-dimension.

In earlier Transmissions you learned about my birth from the Sun and of the relationship between the Radiation Belts and the Sun's energies which produced the specific needs for my expansion of consciousness.

Throughout the Universe, the Galaxies and Star Systems and their planets are all connected with each other in consciousness by crystalline rays of energies. These crystalline rays carry information and Light throughout all dimensions instantaneously. All the planets in the Universe have frequency scales which differ from each other. Often you will find similarities between two planets, however, they do not have the same frequency, just as no two individuals have the same frequency as they manifest their consciousness on my dimension.

My first rays of consciousness were born after my rotatory movement reversed in contrast to the Sun. Up to that time my consciousness mirrored the Sun. With the condensing of my form into greater density I began to develop specific biological material on my surface. Initially, this occurred in the watery part of my surface, and later on the dry land. Trees and other vegetation became antennae which capture transmissions of Light and Information from the various parts of the Galaxy and Universe. Not only do they receive information, but they also act as transmitters by which I can send information to other planets in this Solar System as well as the Galaxy. All this information travels by the crystal rays in space. So that was how my consciousness began to expand and how I was able to develop more complex organisms.

Originally, the hard crystalline rocks which form my mountains and hard surface, acted as the chief receptors for the frequencies passing through the crystal rays. The crystalline rocks absorb the information and energies, resonating them into the atmosphere surrounding them. Their radiations harmonize with the plants and animals which move through their fields, in turn stimulating the personal energy fields of these plants and creatures. The frequencies created changes to the consciousness of the emerging biological organisms. Initial changes occurred in the oceans, since water mirrors all energy fields within it.

Bacteria became stimulated by this process and began to develop different forms due to the morphogenetic patterns being projected through the Radiation belts by the Sun. As "life" evolved in the oceans, my consciousness began to expand and receive greater Light from Brahman. Later organisms moved from the sea to the land, developing antennae that could receive more intensified levels of information.

I am expressing as much Light and consciousness as you do through your Ego. Not far below my surface, not more than 30cm deep, you will detect an energy flow moving constantly from the southern polarity center to the northern polarity. At each pole these energies are highly concentrated or close together, whereas at the equator they are less concentrated and exist more widely apart. In the higher northern and southern latitudes, the type of plant life is more complex and concentrated in its form than in the equatorial regions.

In the tropical regions the plant life has wide and flat leaves, or as with the palm, the leaves hang down, exposing a greater surface area to the Sun. In colder climates trees have needle-like foliage because the electromagnetic fields are more concentrated in these areas and the trees must concentrate the incoming and outflowing of energy and information. In the tropical regions, the flatter foliage is necessary to capture the more dispersed energies. Because the energy flow moves from the South to the North Pole, all the major lateral root systems of the plants align themselves along the energy lines. When Man indiscriminately plants a tree and does not line the major lateral roots in a south-north direction, the plant will not grow strong and mature, and will become a bad antennae, as it does not convey the energies received into the crystalline grid of my body.

The frequencies received by the leaves are transmitted through the crystalline colloidal structures in the trunks of the trees and stems of the plants through to the lateral root systems where they are aligned to the energy flow through the surface soil. At the poles these energies are transmitted to my central core, which may be likened to the Brain center in my body. The information is radiated from this crystalline center back through all the cells of my body, such cells being the plant and animal bodies, including your bodies.

From these structures additional frequencies are emitted back into space to other planets and stars in the Universe. It is a continual flow of Light and Information which constitutes the frequency of Brahman.

To the Ego mind of Man there is constant speculation

about what exists below my surface. I am too large to be weighed by the "modern scientist", so it is still a guessing game for this intellect. Obviously the imagination runs wild with all kinds of theories, such as that I have a hollow center. I am pleased that it is not so, for after being bombarded over many millennia with meteors and comets, such a fragile shell would have cracked open like an eggshell.

Below my surface mantle are the volcanic gases and lava which act as a cushion against outside shocks, in much the same way as the bodies you project to are cushioned with fatty tissue. As you move deeper into my rocky structure, you will find that it becomes honeycombed and is similar to the bony structure of the body, allowing flexibility in response to the bumps and contusions. Within the center of my being is a central globe structure made of crystalline substance which rotates independently of my outward total motion and at a much faster speed. That is not only because of its smaller size, but also because of its different frequency. Its rotational movement creates alternating energy fields radiating through to my surface antennae.

Within this crystalline central sphere exists the pure essence of my Being, which is of my mother Sun, and this allows my constant contact and consciousness with the Sun.

For some Astral reason the Ego consciousness within my bodies seems to assume that consciousness always exists extant somewhere "within" something. They assume that their consciousness exists somewhere in their heart, or within their pineal gland or elsewhere. Consciousness is a flow frequency. It flows through the Ego to the Fourth-dimensional chakras, then to the Etheric chakras, the glands and finally the brain center where all information is processed. With me, consciousness flows from the stars and planets in the Galaxy to my trees and animal bodies, to my central core essence.

Your Egos are connected to the various Star Systems throughout the Galaxy. From there, consciousness flows through the Sun to your Egos and into the Earth-body consciousness. How can your Ego pretend to be more attached to Light than I, for all comes from the same source, only flowing through different resonators - all is Brahman.

In the early stages of my growth, the frequencies which were received by my mountains and plant life eventually became limited in their ability to receive expanded information. However they did extend the field of consciousness to the degree where I was able to attract additional morphogenetic patterns which extended the range of frequencies I was able to receive.

During intervening periods many things occurred as life forms from other planets in the Solar System arrived. Astral interference in this Solar System was well underway for some long while before my atmosphere was troubled by it. In particular, the planet you call Mars was much affected, in a similar way to what is happening to me now. Life forms originating there arrived and were subsequently marooned, failing to survive. However, much of their genetic substance was absorbed into my consciousness and stored in the PSI memory banks in the Radiation Belts.

When the Astral Lords were forced onto my scene, my body forms were still what may best be described as primitive. As you were told in the early Transmissions, the Astral Lords attempted to move their consciousness into my early forms, but they could not survive the separation and density of the Dimension. Their initial attempt did create a taint, one which has helped tie the Egos to the body and the web of their Illusion.

167

Enter the Vortex as One Light

Through continued morphogenesis, I was able to ground higher frequencies of Light which allowed the flow of consciousness from the Fourth and Fifth-dimensions to enter my Being. That was when you commenced your projection from the Galaxy through our Sun. These projections caused a heightened expansion to my consciousness, allowing me to craft my own Light Body on the Fourth-dimension, and that will soon be completed.

Through the Transmissions of Zadore, you are reawakening your latent dimensional frequencies which you turned your back on when your Ego entered the Astral Illusion. For me, the development of your bodies became the final link which allowed the frequencies of the Fourth-dimension to flow through my consciousness from the Galaxy through your Egos. For me it is not a reawakening, but a new growth and movement into the higher dimensional consciousness, as I am becoming one with the Light Consciousness of the Galaxy.

The newly formed Egos allowed Light of such intensity to flow that I began to build my Fourth-dimensional frequencies. The Astral Lords perceived this occurance with alarm, for prior to the influx of Light through your Egos they did not view my growing consciousness as any threat to their plans of control. They had considered my Fourth-dimensional consciousness to be primitive by their standards.

Your developed Egos were for them the way by which they could move back into the higher dimensions, away from their lowly position in the Fourth-dimension. Your Egos are tuned to that frequency which can move Light to and from the Fifth-dimension. It has, then, become a covetous prize for the Astral Lords, to can gain complete control over your Egos, as they believe that by attaching their frequencies to the Egos, they can move their consciousness into the Fifth-dimension and

168

Earth Consciousness

other Star Systems in the Galaxy.

By denying me this Light, the Astral Lords felt that they would also slow down my ascension into the Fourth-dimension. To some extent they have been successful, however, they have never fully captured the Ego, for they have only transferred a few to their dark state. These are the Astral Entities who work through my Bodies to destroy the Light flowing through you. Much of the Light of Brahman has continued to flow into the Third-dimension, however it is often dispersed without meaning, and more often it has been corrupted by the illusionary maneuvers of the Astrals.

Earlier Transmissions from Zadore told how the Astral Lords are continually using their lackeys in government, military and commerce to disrupt the flow of the Galactic frequencies, often by detonating nuclear devices on specific nodal points on my surface. They know that this will affect the resonant harmonic flow of energy and information to corresponding nodal points within the Galaxy. Others are continually destroying the forests and limiting my antennae and contact with the Galaxy. They will stop at nothing in their attempt to move back through to the higher dimensions, creating disharmony and disruption to the flow of Light.

Of all the Vorticies moving through my Being, the Vortex of Zadore is currently emmiting those frequencies which are energizing my surface antennae, and these rejuvenated antennae are beginning to assist in creating greater awareness to the transmitting Egos on the Fourth-dimension. The more who turn away from all illusion, the more Egos will begin to harmonize my body with Light, and this influx of Light will create a dimensional shift in my consciousness, one which will alter forever the present morphogenetic life forms on my surface. It will set the stage for the influx of new morphogenetic forms which will be totally different from the present patterns that you, and the other frequencies of consciousness are using for the expression of My Light.

In fact, all vegetation and animal forms will change to relate to the higher dimensional frequencies flowing through my Being. This new morphogenesis will attract Light from the Fifth-dimension which will continue for many millions of years through my continued growth in the Galaxy. And I, too, will be a Star Frequency like my mother Sun.

For many thousands of years many of the current vegetation and animal bodies will continue to exist side by side with the new forms, just as some of the older plants still exist today. My crystalline mountains will become more fluid and will reflect great Light from the other Systems in the Galaxy. My new morphogenetic forms will be of an Etheric nature, for my whole Being is moving into the higher levels of the Fourth-dimension.

And what of those Astrals? They are now working frantically to stop the flow of Light which is increasing through your deepening consciousness. Their time loop is beginning to corrupt, and unless they can create a major catastrophe to destroy the bulk of bodies on my surface, they will be sucked into greater density and will lose all control over Light and Power. They too could repent, for Brahman is all Light and forgiveness. Brahman does not condemn or blame their actions, for Brahman accepts all. The choice is theirs, and no matter what it is, they will return to Brahman. They can return to the Light with humility, or as primal matter, ready to be reformed in Brahman's Consciousness.

Unfortunately, in all change there appears to be suffering. However, suffering is only experienced in the Astral Illusion. Your Light and Essence will never suffer, and will never be destroyed. Even if your consciousness is temporarily severed from my body, through death, it will return once more to me in the new morphogenesis. For we are all one in Brahman, and, like you, I also thrill at the flow of Love as it passes through my frequency as Light.

Be One with me in Light and Love.

Interlude

There are some people who have read "One Light" and questioned whether it is a book of channelled information. Channelling is fast becoming big business, not only in this country, but throughout the Western World. Many of the "New Age" magazines which you pick up on the news-stands have ads inviting individuals to attend seminars, or to take courses in learning how to become a "channel", or to listen to the advice of some famous "channeller".

This type of endeavour is fraught with danger. In delving into what can best be described as the "old paradigm", unsuspecting individuals open their consciousness to all those seedy entities who dwell in the lower Astral frequencies, and who are constantly awaiting to express their "superior" knowledge on the Third-dimension. None of what they have to say is new, for it is old recycled garbage that can be found in any book in any large library.

Enter the Vortex as One Light

Many of the older writings have referred to channelling as "possession". Those individuals who give freely of their consciousness to these outside entities are diminishing their contact with their own Light and are creating severe karmic effects in their lives now and in the future. In the Christian Bible, there are several references to Jesus casting out devils. These devils are those disincarnate entities who are "partying-on" in the channeller's body and consciousness. Unfortunately in this wonderful "new age" there are many entities who are vampiring the young people who are beginning to open their consciousness, seeking their inner Light. These entities feel that, by creating the impression that channelling is legal and good, they will draw the energies of their followers to their money making plans.

My publisher, in Australia, is involved in the healing profession and he has told me how he has performed metabolic nutritional tests on people who purport to be channels. Apparently they record high deficiency levels of vitamins and minerals in their bodies after a channelling session. In fact, these sessions often leave them tired and drained for some days. Over a period of years this situation begins to create detrimental effects to their immune systems. Apparently one such channel admitted that he always felt this way after a session but did not see that there was any permanent danger to his health. He also said that *he* (the guide) was demanding on his time for he never knew when the guide would want to speak. Like Shamans, who, it is well known, are often reluctant to take up the practice of Shamanism at first because of the detrimental effect it will have on the health of their close relatives, channellers often draw on the energies of others who live near and with them, and, in a sense, "vampire" them, knowingly or unknowingly.

The Transmissions I am receiving through Zadore are

173

not in any way related to channelling. They are a flow of information from being One Light. What you need to understand is that everyone on this planet considers that they are an individual. They are born into a body from the Earth, and they believe that this consciousness which they experience in that body makes them unique apart from everything and everyone else in the Universe. They are correct in that they are expressing individual rays of Light through the Ego and body, however they feel that they are that body, and that they are John Smith or Mary Smith, or whoever, for they are allowing their Ego to demand that they have an identity here on the Third-dimension.

They are asleep to just who and what they are. When I first discovered the capsule, I was unaware that Zadore was actually "Me" - the true ME. I felt quite separate in my Ego from Zadore, and later Sizzond. Once I began to move away from all Astral influence on my Ego, especially when Razparil was unable to approach the Light of Sizzond, there was an increased flow of Light through my Ego. For I am becoming that which I truly am - Sizzond Zadore - One Light.

This is not channelling but is speaking from your own Light, for you become what you are - a Being of Light. Until this occurred I was not able to translate these Transmissions into language that can be understood on this Dimension. Do not ever consider becoming a channel of the Astrals, but work to becoming one with the Light which you are, for that will illuminate your consciousness daily. It will be your "Zadore", your "Zarine". You will need no books to teach you, because you are a self- illuminating being and one with Brahman.

It is interesting to share with you at this time something special. We have found that everyone who has read "One Light" has been profoundly moved by its message of freedom. The Transmissions in "One Light" triggered a memory within each person's consciousness that they are already a Being of Light, and it is time to awaken from the illusionary sleep. The message empowers each and every individual to be that Light. For too long, Astral control has sought to bring individuals together in a group to find power and knowledge in a shared manner. They know that once two or more gather in such endeavours then they (the Astrals) are immediately present in that group. In all instances the group develops rules and procedures to hold it together. All that follows is the creation of a leader for the movement and it becomes completely Ego dominated, and consequently becomes fully Astral.

The flight to One Light is the flight back to expressing the beauty and light which is YOU, for you then begin to realize this and express it. You have no need for a support group, since if you did you would be tempted to express your Ego tendencies.

Do you see the simplicity of what One Light is? To be and express your Light, you automatically affect all those with whom you come into contact, whether it is a personal contact, or a contact through writing, painting, singing or any way of expressing your love for the Earth and Brahman. The purity of your intention reaches into others and they begin to feel stirrings within their own inner being which will begin to awaken their own Light.

Zadore has given these Transmissions to reach into your Being and resonate the information with your Light, for this resonating energy will harmonize your feelings, and those feelings will demand attention from your Ego.

Do not become fasciniated with external mirrored light. Many individuals constantly find pleasure with all the Astral toys, as they feel these toys hold the secret that will unleash personal power within them. They feel that if they can "see" auras; perform Astral travel; develop occult power; use psychic powers to impress others; perform miraculous healings; and use gems to create deeper meditative states, then they are expressing their inner Light. While you look without, you will never find the truth, for all outward direction only leads to Astral Illusion. There is nothing wrong with possessing these additional skills, however when all is said and done, they are of no more benefit to developing inner spirituality than are your five body senses, because in most cases they are only an extension of the senses, as these new skills belong to the Etheric and lower Astral bodies.

Do not fear the coming changes which the Earth has just told you of in the last Transmission, for nothing can harm you but the fear itself. Your body is of the Earth, and as such will always return to its mother. Your inner being is not of this Third-dimension, so whatever occurs with the energy frequencies of the planet will in no way harm you. Do not allow the doomsday-sayers to influence your consciousness. There is no programmed Armageddon; it is only a figment of fear placed in the consciousness by the Astral Entities through their mischievous writings. So constantly do they flood the ethers with the fear of its happening, that they have convinced the mass of humanity that it will occur, and that belief in the occurence will help precipitate some damaging affects to the Human Race. Also, any natural changes of the Earth will be characterized as being part of this "terrifying" event. These Transmissions will move your consciousness away from such Astral concepts and back to Light.

Initially in this book, you were told that the Vortex from Zadore has been moving Light energy into this dimension since November 1995. The Earth is constantly harmonizing the energies of the Vortex as it moves through its crystalline structure into all the plant and animal bodies, and this includes the human body. Although you may not realize it, these frequencies are drawing your consciousness deeper into the Earth vibration, and aligning your Ego closer to the pure flow of Light, which is YOU.

Do not make this Book of Transmissions just an intellectual pursuit, for it is important that you feel the energies flowing through your body and Ego consciousness every hour of the day. Follow the Transmissions in the sequence that they are written in this book, and they will act as keys that will open doorways within your consciousness. As you journey through these Transmissions you are moving through the Vortex. There will never be any One Light Center, for if there is ever an organization by that name, or any such similar one, know that it is Astrally motivated. Such an organization, if you involve yourself in it, will only defeat the opening to your One Light.

Continue your journey through these Transmissions to discover your own Light and personal freedom. This is the only path for everyone. Do not become distracted with statements like, "There are many paths which lead toward personal salvation." This is an Astral ploy. There is only One Path and only One Light, as Brahman is One. Your path is currently involved in assisting the Ascension of the Earth.

Transmission
Fifteen

Informational Pathways

Your Ego feels a strong attachment to your Earth-body for it has, for many thousands of years, moved its energies through many bodies on this dimension. Very rarely do you stop and feel the frequencies of Light flowing through your Ego to the Earth-body, and out through your five body senses into the Third-dimensional consciousness on the Earth sphere. In your semi-sleep state each day you vaguely accept this flow of consciousness and Light and call it "life". It represents your life as well as the life of all other beings passing through your conscious field.

Mostly you accept this "life" as your experience, as well as it being an unchangeable condition - something you were born into, to move through, ending with the death of the body. For some of you it seems purposeless - a time of suffering,

178

Informational Pathways

whilst others seek a purpose in being here. Often an individual purpose, or suffering, appears to be aligned to external events such as massive changes in consciousness in the community, be they environmental, scientific, political or industrial. There is a reaction occurring between Earth changes and personal karma, and both shape the life achievement. Others patiently await the death of their body, as they are led to believe that through this release they will go to some paradise free from the torments of Third-dimensional life.

The five senses of the body are the informational pathways for all consciousness to pass through from the highest dimensions out into the Third-dimension. For it is the Earth and its consciousness which are interacting with this total flow of Light and information. All understanding and use of this information and Light received by the Earth is either returned back through the five informational channels to the higher dimensions, or radiated out into the Third-dimensional Universe.

The pathways can become blocked by an override of information processed by the Ego as it moves information through the Illusion to the Astral Lords. That is, it is moved through the Ego "lens" to the Astral level on the Fourth-dimension. What occurs is that much of the information destined for the Earth is redirected by the Ego to the Astral dimension. It is then recycled back through the Illusionary Web to the Ego and to the Earth through the five pathways. Thus the Astrals have been able to create and maintain their "Time Loop" on the Third-dimension, which holds the consciousness of the Egos and their attachment to the Earth-bodies in the continual repetitive life patterns.

Should you lose all contact with the five sensual pathways, your Ego consciousness will be unable to manifest any form of consciousness on the Third-dimension. This occurs at the time of the death of the body and often in cases where the neural pathways are destroyed and one lays in a coma for many years. Unable to react with the energies of the dimension, the comatose person is then termed "a vegetable", which is incorrect, for plants are living conscious entities constantly interacting with their environment. Many people are asleep to their true state and follow a monotonous pattern of existence, never really coming close to their source of Light and information. They live and exist not much differently to the vegetable, for they work solely through body consciousness and react constantly to the physical forces which seem to control their lives. Living on this frequency, they believe that only what they can touch and see is real, and this constitutes their conscious acceptance of the forces that control the Illusion.

Do you truly know what your Earth-body actually looks like? Your whole concept of your body revolves around the reflection you see in a mirror. After some years you believe that mirror reflection to be you. However, when you look at a photograph of yourself or see a video, you deny that it is a correct likeness of you, as to your Ego consciousness these do not match with the reflection in the mirror. Others say that the photograph is a true likeness of how they see you, but inwardly you do not accept it, for you know that the camera result does not portray your image as YOU see it. The reflection in your mirror, however, is interactive with the vanities of the Ego and is constantly colored by the way you see yourself, as your Ego expects to see itself relative to its own mental picture of what it expects others to see. For instance, it may appreciate certain looks and mannerisms of some film star, business person or athlete, and although its body does not possess these attributes, it feels it does, and when looking into a mirror, it masks its vision into believing it sees what it expects to see. This is living deeply in the Illusion. The Ego imagines it is learned, loving to others, attractive, appealing, and many other vanities, and it has, since its early attachment with the body, been projecting these pictures out through the five informational pathways and reflecting this image back to itself through the mirror. The Ego expects others in the Third-dimension to instantly recognize these "virtues" which it possesses and which it believes it is radiating outward. This is truly the way of the Astrals.

As the information is moved through the Ego from the higher dimensions, it becomes colored by the vain attitudes of the Ego and passes out into the Third-dimension distorted. So that there are many such Egos expressing their vanities and creating confused messages for the Earth, producing high levels of negative frequencies on the planet.

Constantly, you interact with these other Egos as you move through the dimension daily. Often you are caught up with the same Egos, and are fighting and trying to move them into your projection. You feel that they are behaving to you and others in a particular way, and you begin to judge them and punish them in any form you can. What you do not realize is that often they are unaware of your feelings and intentions, and so react in a particular way which disturbs you. For you are unaware that they are only reflecting your own inner insecurities and behavior back to you. What you see disturbing in another is not actually disturbing to that individual, for in all cases the individual is unaware of his or her behavior and sees your interaction as being aggressive in return. This confused and mixed reaction is generally explained as bad "chemistry".

When individual Egos reach a certain degree of power and accomplishment within the Illusion, they begin to work to establish a permanent existence for their Egos, one which will be recorded in history for all time. If such an Ego is a leader of a government, he or she will attempt to make changes for the people in a dramatic way. If a king or an autocrat, he erects monuments or pyramids; in business, he or she will mold an empire which may last several generations. These Egos do this because inwardly they fear that they do not actually "exist", and on the death of their physical body "they" will disintegrate into millions of pieces just as the elements of the body are returned to the earth. They feel that "they" will continue to exist in the memory of all others yet to come, and somehow this gives them eternal life. From this you will appreciate how an Ego caught in the Illusion will not move the best energies through the informational pathways to the Earth and the other Earth-bodies.

As you now realize, many individuals use the sensual pathways as an outlet for their Egos to dominate and control others through misuse of the information passing through their senses. They reinforce the Illusion on the Earth by projecting through the dimension those concepts that other people will accept as constituting "life" and how life should be lived. As you move your Ego away from the Illusion you will clearly see how the Astral entities are cleverly projecting these control mechanisms into the consciousness of the mass of humanity in order to enslave the Egos and consciousness and chain them to a constant return to the Third-dimension.

In your current unfoldment and movement away from the Astral Illusion, you are not fully conscious of the Third-dimension, and are not able to move all your energies to the Earth. You still live in some respects within the parameters of the Illusion, and you do not consciously utilize all the five informational pathways. Basically, you focus on one or two at a time and it is only when you become involved with an attack on your body that all pathways will function together. You may be stalked by a killer, or an animal, or you may be involved in fighting in a war zone, and at such times you are on full sense alert. At most other times the senses lay dormant, only to be aroused through certain emotional stimulus. At various periods during your day your consciousness moves through various frequencies, depending on the development of your Ego. Mostly you move through the levels of the Third-dimension and into the two lowest levels of the Fourth-dimension.

As you are not able to be fully conscious of what your Third-dimensional body looks like, how then is it possible for you to have any concept of what your Fourth or Fifth-dimensional being looks like? The imagination of Mankind is a powerful attribute and individuals continually build pictures of what they consider higher dimensional beings should resemble. Just look at the imaginative pictures used to portray beings from other planets and star systems. However, all the imagination does here is transpose a Third-dimensional form to other levels, and the easiest way for it to create an understandable image is to picture that form as being less dense than the ones it knows.

All the Dimensions of Brahman are composed of different frequencies, and the form which is needed on the Third-dimension is different from those needed on the Fourth and higher dimensions. Because of the density of the frequencies of the Third-dimension, the body is constructed with legs, arms and five informational pathways which are needed for consciousness to manifest at that level.

Why then, on another dimension, would you need Third-dimensional form and pathways? The Earth-body's form is generated within the Radiation belts from unique morphogenetic patterns. This body form did not just occur, rather it was a progression of biological changes over many millions of years. The changes grounded higher frequencies from the Galaxy and the Higher dimensions.

Enter the Vortex as One Light

As you learned in the Earth Transmission, future morphogenetic body forms will differ from the current body pattern, for as the frequencies of the Earth change, so too will bodies, as they need to receive higher vibrational information required for the progression of the Earth's consciousness.

All morphogenetic patterns used by the Earth over the many millions of years will be retained in the Earth's memory banks in the Radiation belts, as they will be used when the Earth moves into the Fifth-dimension and creates its own Third-dimensional planet.

Your Earth-body form is connected to other frequencies which move through the higher levels of the Third-dimension up to the two lower levels of the Fourth-dimension. These lower Fourth-dimensional levels are inhabited by the Astral Lords and by many other Egos who are awaiting a new Earth experience. All this is occurring on the second level, for the first level is saturated with the karmic pool of the Earthly experience of many Egos as well as the negative thought forms created by you during your Earth experiences.

Once you are able to move your consciousness to the higher levels of the Fourth-dimension, with the aid of the Vortex, you will no longer need a morphogenetic form similar to your Third-dimensional Earth-body. You will not need the five informational pathways on this and higher levels of consciousness, for they are only the tools of the Third-dimension.

On the higher dimensions there is basically one pathway which expresses the five sensual expressions of the Earth-body, and this is best described in Third-dimensional language as "feeling", for in Light, feeling and its associated energies are radiated out into the dimensions. The upper levels of the Fourth-dimension radiate a high intensity of pure Light, and the form for consciousness resembles a sphere of light and energy moving out throughout the dimension, interconnecting with all other Light spheres of consciousness. These spheres of dimensional Light follow the patterns of Brahman similar to the Stars in the Third-dimension.

It is extremely difficult for you to imagine a Fourth-dimensional form when you do not clearly see your own Third-dimensional form. When Sizzond appeared to your consciousness, Jon, you had no other option than to mirror your picture and feeling of what you inwardly expected a being of such Light intensity should be. In other words you did not perceive any form, just Light and a communication through consciousness, then using the multitude of memory patterns inherent in your Ego, you gave Sizzond form. That is how all contact with higher dimensional Beings has been recorded by people on the Third-dimension throughout the ages. It is important for you to meditate on this and expand your consciousness beyond Third - dimensional concepts of what something should or should not look like. To do this you will move higher energy frequencies to the Earth and dispel many of the erroneous concepts about other beings.

When I move consciousness through the lower levels of my being, the Ego attempts to portray my frequencies in some material form. I first need to slow down the Light frequencies through Sizzond, and further to the Ego and finally to my Earth-body, for that is how you are receiving these Transmissions. Adjustments are constantly made on all levels in order that the brain can translate concepts into thoughts and words. I have never expressed my Fifth-dimensional form on the Third-dimension, for that is an impossibility. By now, Jon, you should know that your body and Ego consciousness is my informational pathway into the Third-dimension.

It is correct for you to assume that my downward flow

passes through the two lower levels of the Fourth-dimension, however the information is not corrupted by the influences on the two lower levels because your Ego is turned away from there and joined with Sizzond. It is in this way that the Vortex also passes through the lower levels of the Fourth-dimension, and the more who study these Transmissions and begin to live through them, the more pure Light will flow through the informational pathways of the Third-dimension.

On the second level of the Fourth-dimension the Astral Illusion reigns supreme, and anything that your mind can conceive at that frequency it can have. You can be a God, an angel, a millionaire, a king or queen; in fact this Illusion lulls your consciousness into being able to suffer no more, and your weakened sensual pathways into a sleep-like state.

Whilst your consciousness is operating on the Third-dimension the Astral Lords continually brainwash it into believing that the Earth is a place of suffering, and that you are there because of the misdeeds of your forefathers or your own misdeeds in former lives. And that your only way to freedom is by following strict dogma and rules laid down by their various cults which are designed to allow your entry into blissful states after the death of your body. However, now, the old heaven has been replaced with something more in keeping with the current consciousness on the planet. Nevertheless, although it is couched in "New Age" concepts, it still provides the same result for the Astrals.

In the "New Age", the Astrals have merged some of the old Eastern concepts with Christian mysticism, and logically assert that the only way you will attain their degree of consciousness is to constantly return to Earth and perfect your soul. For the Astrals, having everyone believe that it is necessary to constantly return in order to work off Karma, is a victory. They know that each time more Karma will be created, for during every life experience you will make some mistakes which will tie you into the return. The Astrals play on human weakness, a weakness which often prevents the attainment of perfection.

The information flow passing through the Vortex will push aside all these negative blocks to your consciousness and allow you to take control and be just who and what you are, for you certainly have no need to continually follow the Astral Illusion. Accept your freedom now, and be.

There will be a time when you will perceive your form or being, and that will occur when you reflect the Light of Brahman, since that is what you are. You will only see what you are when you reflect back to your consciousness what you project outward. When you move away from this Dimension, either after the death of your Earth-body or through deep states of attunement when still on the Third-dimension, you will ground your consciousness on another Dimension. Consciousness, being what it is, will flow through that new dimension, and through that flow you will become aware of your form as it expresses itself on that dimension. That is what I referred to when talking about Sizzond when you awakened to his consciousness.

Consciousness manifests on all levels through the out-flow of Love of Brahman. The word "love" is filled with many different meanings in the consciousness of the Third-dimension, and in itself does not completely allow you to understand or feel YOU.

On a Third-dimensional level, the best description of You - Brahman working through You - is a feeling of "Warmth". You have this feeling when you appreciate the actions another person performs selflessly on your behalf. This Warmth flows right through your five sensual pathways. It flows when you have close feelings and relationships with others, and when you feel joy for the achievements of others, for it is the Light of Brahman moving through Its creation. You cannot mentally choose this flow of Warmth, or have it on demand, for it is only experienced by feeling your Light flowing through a purified Ego, and radiating out to all.

Always I have encouraged you to develop this inner feeling, for the more you attune to this inner feeling, the more Warmth will be experienced by you and others in your field of work on the Third-dimension.

This Warmth moves through all dimensions and is the creative energy of Brahman. The intense heat from the Sun creates Warmth throughout all the Solar System, and all the other Stars in the Universe continually emit Light and Warmth for the glory of Brahman. It is a deep nourishing force which flows through all things and all beings, and it constantly flows through you. Become aware of its Warmth and Presence, and kindle its flames as it expands through your whole Being.

Constantly, you are moving closer to being that which you are, for there are no rules or dogma to come between. Do not expect that there should be a continual flow of karma in your life experience, for you are shedding all old karma continually, and becoming free forever - NOW! Move your Warmth and Light to your Ego, and it will respond to this in preference to the old Astral Illusion. Begin to move with the Earth consciousness as it rejoices in its freedom as well.

Think of this as being a regeneration of your Being, for like your body which requires the expulsion of toxins for its return to health, your karma is your toxin of a higher frequency and it requires effort to cast it off. So that, like the body, your Ego will return to its pristine state, working in One Light. No doubt you will temporarily suffer discomfort, especially that of giving up the old vanities and distorted pictures of your self importance in the Illusion of life. This will last for a remarkably short time and you will surface in a peace and freedom that you have never dreamed existed.

Why wait and relive many more life experiences on the Earth when you can choose your freedom NOW!

It is as simple as that, for it is only the Astral Illusion and the system imbedded within it which tells you otherwise.

The more you feel the "Warmth" flowing within your consciousness, the more quickly you will become YOU FOR-EVER!

Transmission
Sixteen

The Power of the
Moment

How often do you feel helpless - helpless in your efforts to change the events of the world which are being impressed constantly on your consciousness through the newspapers and television? Some of you are experiencing greater difficulties than others as you are caught in the crossfire of waring sections of your community, for around you exists the constant murder, pillage and destruction of life, and the feeling that the world is worse now than it was several generations ago.

This helplessness only leads to despair, and the resultant suffering forces your consciousness back to the Astral Gods in the vain hope that they will punish the perpetrators. However, those who are conducting the rape of humanity are doing so in the name of their own particular God. What of you who live in the "safe" countries, do you not sometimes feel guilt and helplessness, knowing that your government supports the manufacture and sale of armaments which are used to further inflame wars in other lands?

How often do you cry out, "What can I do to change what is occurring?" Individuals who work in the manufacture of weapons of destruction condone what is being done in the name of sales and profits, otherwise they would not continue working in the pay of these agents of murder. It is a lame excuse to say "I need the money to support my family," for he or she who says that is as bad as the masters who pay them - they cannot escape the responsibility of their actions!

Changes of Government, and altered ideologies, only change the reason for the killing of the many bodies of the Earth, and not only the bodies of the humans but also the other animals and vegetation.

You cry out as one amongst the billions on the planet and you see no way to alter what is occurring, then the feeling is submerged back into your unconscious, being placed in the "too hard" basket. However, what is suppressed will again surface to haunt you. You have that inner feeling that you are important, however you are unable to bring that feeling directly into your daily consciousness. It exists in the back of your mind and you follow your daily circle of activities, often expecting that, somehow, you will discover the key which will unlock some power within you and you will break free from all that is happening. The statement, "No man is an island," is true and you cannot divorce your life from the Earth and its inhabitants. Becoming "bored" with the "sameness" of your life, or frustrated with your inability to discover that importance you truly seek, you lose yourself for a time by becoming engrossed in a fantasy on the movie screen, or play computer games and indulge in virtual reality. All such activities only draw you deeper into the Illusion of the Astrals.

You now become cemented in your body, believing that it is really you, and you accept its natural cycle of ageing and decay as being your cycle of destruction. With the ending of the body cycle, within your consciousness you hope for some freedom at the end of your journey.

Some ask, "Is that all there is?" accepting the death of the body as the end of their consciousness. They reaffirm this as, "You only live once!"

It is important that you continually study all these Transmissions and master the changes in consciousness which they are leading you to. This is the way by which you will be able to break free of the Astral control on your Ego. These Transmissions are being moved through Jon, and both Jon and Rose are writing them for you, so that you too can experience true freedom on all dimensions. You, in turn, should make the Transmissions more available to others who you know are also struggling to be free. For the Transmissions are meant for **Everyone** on the planet, as the Earth requires all its consciousness to move with it to the Fourth-dimension. Those who are not prepared to move will lose their bodies and return to the Astral Dimension. Feel inspired by your freedom and allow your Light to direct these teachings to all others.

The Transmissions are destined for all humanity and not only for those living in a stable "safe" economy. All bodies on the Earth are the Earth's bodies and part of its consciousness. There is no need for missionaries in this work, as once your Light is exposed into the Third-dimensional plane, it will affect others who move through your field of Light, and as you

192

enhance the consciousness of the Earth by radiating the warmth and love of Brahman, others will be affected by you.

No matter where your Earth-body is, you can and will move energy to the Earth, for you will be constantly attuned to the information flowing through the Vortex of Light and Healing, for you are an expression of Brahman.

No matter where you are or what you do, you will express Light if you focus your consciousness away from your Ego and the Illusion.

Originally, the Astral Lords moved the frequency of fear into the primitive organisms on the Earth. For many thousands of years following they used this frequency to control the consciousness moving through those organisms. In order to capture and enslave the consciousness of early humanity, the Astral Lords created, in the dream state of the people, visions of Gods and Goddesses. Because of the nature of the Astral Lords, these God-visions were not kind and peaceful or high-minded, but were murderous and lustful and were constantly at war with one another. These Gods abounded in human consciousness throughout the world and infested every society.

In order that the messages and commands of the Gods should be successfully purveyed to the society of men in an organized and controlled way, an earthly individual was needed to transmit the information. Such individuals are marked throughout the recorded and un-recorded history of the races and tribes. These were the priest-Kings, "the high priests", the auguries, and witch doctors who held the God's ear. Later on, when in some areas of the world the Gods departed, the Oracles came and spoke to Kings through the priests and priestesses of the temples. It needed no great power to be a transmitter of the guiding information of the races, for this was no different to the "channelling" activities of your current century. They were and are the channels of the misconceptions and the control patterns of the Astral Lords.

But the Oracles ceased and the numbers of the Gods declined, and this was due to a shift in the Earth's consciousness as its Etheric frequencies began to interconnect its consciousness more closely to the Sun. This shift forced a change in the Astral concept, for the Astral Lords found that humanity was closely aligned with the Earth's consciousness and the closer relationship with the Sun created a concept of a One God in the race consciousness, thereby excluding many Gods.

So then, the Astral Lords found that they could follow this concept by addressing the focus of all energy to the One God idea. In fact, this proved a more efficient method of drawing greater energy, concentrating it to one source rather than scattering it to many Gods. Old habits die hard, and many Astral Lords who had enjoyed being Gods and vampiring energies from the ignorant Egos of Mankind, found their answer in becoming "Masters" able to work in concert with the One God. Quite readily, they gave to themselves grandiose names and titles, as even now they do, whilst claiming to serve the Nameless God. And yet how many names of this God abound! Aten; Jehovah; Allah etc. Even Jesus, the Christ has become a God! How cleverly they have exploited his life and work so that he is worshiped as a God by the mass of humanity when actually this was not his purpose at all.

The Astral Lords still move their consciousness to Mankind by accessing the hindbrain during the sleep time of any individuals who leave their body consciousness open to intrusion. That is why I taught you how to protect your consciousness and body prior to sleeping each night. They use the imagery which the old brain accepted thousands of years ago and which is submerged not very far below the conscious level of the mind of Man. It still forms an actual zone of consciousness on the lowest level of the Fourth-dimension; it is the region of Karma as well as of all the dross that Man dumps there during continued states of negativity. Being a frequency of such density of darkness and negativity, it is the realm entered by people who have accumulated Karma over many lives and who have no intention of lessening it, and wish to use the energies over unsuspecting people, to dominate them and use them as their servants to accomplish their nefarious ends. The Astral Lords in turn have used these dark entities to further their ends, and many of these beings have become Astral Entities.

To these Entities, the Astral Lords have revealed many of the "secrets" of the energy functions of the Earth and its consciousness, and the Entities have been able to manipulate matter to their advantage in order to seek power over other human beings who are easily influenced by temporal greatness.

The Fear frequency is the greatest tool that the Astral Lords and their Entities use to control human consciousness and events on the Earth, for this Fear frequency permeates every cell of your body. How often do you move into this Fear frequency? You do so when you feel that your body is under some threat, or when someone discovers your misdeeds and you fear ruination of your name and reputation. The fear of such consequences often drives some individuals to suicide, as they feel that by this they will escape the consequences of their actions.

Once you uncover this Fear as being nothing more than a mechanism instilled into the body by the Astrals as a vehicle for their own protection, then you will easily be able to create those frequencies which will remove this frequency from your consciousness and your body, also freeing the Earth from this toxic waste.

It is time that you discover your own personal power,

and learn how not to be intimidated by and be powerless in the face of the Astral plot to manipulate you through constant wars and economic depressions, which make you dependent on their Entities who deceive you into believing that they are your hope and salvation. Accept the greatness of your Being as it exists outside the Illusion. You can do this NOW! Even if you are currently living under the oppression of these Entities in your country. Listen to this Transmission and learn the Power of the Moment!

This certainly is not your first life-experience, for you have projected into Earth-bodies for many thousands of years. You have had many different experiences, some of which were seen as good and others which can only be described as horrid. You have murdered, raped and committed all kind of atrocities over many of your life experiences. When you do not recognize this you tend to hold yourself up as judge and jury of those who currently commit themselves to such practices. Your Ego does not want to be seen as being cruel or evil, so it cloaks itself under a veil of deception and illusion. This is how your basic karma hides from your consciousness.

If you desire wealth and fame, position and power, you will attract those frequencies that will lead you toward the experience of those desires, for the more you focus in that direction, the more deeply will you move into the Illusion, and become a servant of the Astral Lords.

Possibly, you now find yourself living in humble surroundings, and inwardly you yearn for more wealth and a grander lifestyle. In past life experiences you lived in such circumstances where you had everything that you could desire, but that never led you to freedom.

Should you now battle constantly with your past urges and let them sway your consciousness, then you will be stressed, always trying to attain the unattainable. For your Light Essence will not allow your Ego to repeat the same experience which it regards as fruitless. Prior to your moving your Ego and consciousness into this current Earth-body, you decided that you had no further need for the power and falsity of the Illusion, so do not let the energy of those past life-experiences procrastinate your movement into Light now. You are now advancing toward expressing that Light which flows from Brahman into this body of the Earth.

Discover now the power of living the moment. Do not focus on the past, neither the past of this life nor of other lives' experiences - you have nothing more to learn from the past, for it is YOU NOW! You are a total expression of all that is you NOW. There is no need to be sorrowful for those actions which you committed in the past, and if you are suffering at this time be aware that this suffering is only the end result of all that was wrongly expressed by you in the past, because it is a purging karma that is returning you to your One Light and Brahman. Allow your Ego to move through this end point and feel the freedom which is emerging from the experience, for this is your current moment of consciousness, and it is ever changing.

Do not constantly live your future in your mind. Doing so is a normal process in the Illusion, and here everyone is taught that planning and setting goals in the correct way will bring about the desired result. However planning never ends in the way you think because the wants of millions of others always indirectly affect the outcome of your desires. Your Inner Light Consciousness has already predetermined your experience, only you tend to push it aside, your Ego knowing better, basing all on the consensus of the Illusion.

If you decide not to work with the essence of your being but choose to follow the Ego desires, this leads you to more

Enter the Vortex as One Light

Karma and frustration by the end of your journey. Learn to live for the moment and experience its power. Learn to feel and listen and follow the urges that are flowing through you. Await the moment of your frequency in the Universe, for you will do no wrong and experience no pain, for you are all Light and intent.

You have been brainwashed into believing that what you do now will be your future. You desire that your future flows from what you experience now into a period of security and enough money to live out the last of your days comfortably within the Illusion. This is Ego planning and constantly moves your consciousness away from the true Light of your being and deeper into the Illusion, since once you get close to achieving what you planned, it pales into insignificance as you then see brighter baubles for your continuing future.

There is no future, only the continuing now, for you are not moving through time, as all is at one in Brahman, and it is the illusionary mind which perceives progression away from the now. Start rejoicing in the moment of now and feel the changes flowing through all of the different aspects of now, for as you feel and listen, all becomes what is, and your position will change as you experience the dance of life.

Realize there is no need to dwell on the past, allowing your consciousness to become preoccupied with all the wasted projects that led you nowhere in this and past life-experiences. This is one of the great "secrets" of life and I want you to consider what it will mean to you, for it is a part of your freedom.

To live for the moment means that you do what needs to be done - NOW. Nothing in your life is meaningless, all has purpose. Do not neglect the work which seems repetitive and a drudge, because it all fits into the fullness of your life, it is all part of the total picture which you are longing to see.

Remember that, as you live the moment, you will discover that there is no particular future, just the ever-expanding now, and as you move your consciousness into your Light Being and remember yourself, you will see and apprehend the total of you on all dimensions simultaneously. There lies true Freedom and Light.

The more you allow your Light to dominate your consciousness, the greater the flow of energy will pass into your existence and to the Earth.

And do not neglect the "now" of the body that you inhabit. No matter what the state of your health you can improve the function of your body if you try, for the more you look after the health and welfare of your body, the more energy you will be able to convey to the Earth.

The Earth is changing and does not require your Ego to input the Astral frequencies to it, for that is what it is moving away from. Current "New Age" groups are unaware of the Astral frequencies flowing through their messages. Under the guise of Masters and other titles, the Astrals encourage seekers to join together and focus energy to specific frequencies created by Astral Lords. It is often expressed as projecting inner light to the center of the Earth, then out to the Master's frequency beyond the Earth, and then to scatter the light frequencies out into the universe. The Astral Lords use these techniques in order to draw energy from willing humans to strengthen their means of control. If such a procedure was beneficial, then the projected energy would remain with the Earth, where it is needed, and not be channelled beyond into the universe.

All this is occurring within your consciousness and you will only find peace and power in the essence of your own being, for your Light is the Light that is in everyone, only it needs to be discovered.

199

Transmission
Seventeen

And the Band Played On

In your life and in the lives of other human beings who are living their current experience within the Earth's consciousness, is that feeling that all is disordered and directionless. The answer you are constantly given is to take charge of your life, and make things and circumstance occur and be under your control.

In the last Transmission I encouraged you to begin to move your consciousness into living for the moment. To some of you that appeared to be an impossibility. For your Ego uses every moment to program, plan and action those frequencies which continually play on the strings of its consciousness.

What is the Ego doing, and more importantly, why is it leading the dance of your life? Your life, as I have just said, appears to be disordered and in chaos, and if that is how you see it, then it is obvious that you should take steps to rectify the matter. And what appears a better way than to assert the desires of your Ego which seems more in control than you? Why, has it not had a proven track record on this Dimension for many thousands of years?

So you are taught that everything is achievable and ordered through applying the proven methods of thinking. In seeking to accomplish order in your life you will find that there are many experts who are continually expanding the methods of achieving greater power by applying their systems. For instance, you have the "positive" thinking process, the "lateral" thinking, the "dimensional" and "cosmic" methods which will place you above others and provide you with a successful and complete life.

Each process of applied thinking always includes the basic methods of "reason", which are deductive and inductive in their application. To be deductive, you start with a premise or fact and apply reason from that point to it conclusion. By applying inductive reason to those deductions, you are able to bring in past experiences which modify the outcome of the thinking. However the whole reasoning process is designed to produce an "action" on one or more thoughts passing through your Third-dimensional consciousness. Should you add an emotional desire to the thought, then the action seems to become charged with energies that quickly release it into the Dimension for expression.

The flow of thoughts passing into your Third-dimensional consciousness from your Ego is constant and demanding. It may be likened to a bombardment of energy which is scattered throughout your consciousness where you tend to grasp at the one thought which you see will be most beneficial to your future needs. However the result of this is that you are unable to bring any condition to its successful conclusion. This leads to frustration and grabbing at other thoughts moving through your consciousness. Often this behavior reaches such intensity that you become stressed and suffer some sort of illness in the process.

It must be seen that all thinking methods are linked back to the process of reasoning, and it is through applying the deductive and inductive reasoning tools, that you produce the wrong results in all your actions.

You say that there are many individuals who stand out from the mass of humanity who are considered as being successful in their expression in the worldly Illusion. These individuals are no more successful than any one else, they only take more time to cultivate thought into action. In other words, they place the core thought centrally in their consciousness and allow this core essence to attract other thoughts and concepts to it, to fit in with the need for its expression. They do not follow the well trodden path of releasing the thought first into the dimension and then progressively adding factors that are seen to increase its success and deleting those which hinder its advancement. As far as they are capable, they watch their creation in their consciousness expand and grow by integrating into it factors that will be beneficial to its outcome, before they release it into the Dimension for completion.

Are these individuals any more directionally focused than others who just move a thought outward and play with it as it either grows or sinks into nothingness? Are these individuals still not also trapped in the Illusion of the Ego and have only modified an outcome?

Those who appear successful in their lives and accomplishments are often only following one major core desire, and in fact they never really reach the thing which they originally sought. They, too, have not touched the inner consciousness that continually demands attention.

What you must see is that most individuals structure their actions from their thoughts in line with many of the tenets expressed by the Astral Illusion. By this I mean that they prefer to base the desired outcome relative to some illusionary outcome. They may desire to achieve wealth, security in old age, or to be an important person in government or a profession. Others align their actions to fit in with a religious or philosophical concept and so forth. One of the major illusionary actions tends to flow with the many prophesies which are widely touted in the Illusion. The current "New Age" movement has been impinged upon by many negative Astral concepts, and by individuals who find that they can make many dollars from sincere seekers who are moving from flower to flower, trying to find the absolute truth in their life now.

Many are unable to find their higher consciousness, for there are countless and varied systems who hold themselves as the way to take you there. These have, over many thousands of years, effectively brainwashed you into believing that your "soul" is something separate from you and that somehow you have to find it and save it. You are told that this nebulous soul was made by God just for you; that, being separate, your task is to save it from being enslaved by the devil or Satan. You are constantly instructed that only by giving your total devotion to this God will you be able to save this soul. Why does it need to be saved? And what does it need to be saved from? If this soul is of the same essence as God, then how can any such subservient being such as a devil lay any claim to it?

What has commonly been termed as your "soul" is nothing more than your Ego. It is time to put the worn out concepts of soul, the devil, heaven and hell well out of your consciousness, for they have no part in One Light. The only devil you will find is the Ego which has transgressed and moved away from its own Light essence, and aligned its purposes with the Astral Illusion, and the only Gods it worships under these circumstances are the Astral Lords who promise it all freedom and heavenly gifts. What suffers is the Earth and its consciousness. Do not waste your time in seeking your soul, but first seek the higher light consciousness which is truly you, and turn your Ego to face that Light constantly, for then you will be all and remember all.

Use meditation as a starting point in your quest to remember yourself. Each day enter into an attunement with that which is you. Do not focus on any personality or being outside your consciousness, such as Jesus or Buddha, or even some Astral God, for your higher consciousness is always with you and awaiting your attention. You must constantly move within yourself the experience of this aspect of yourself beyond the Ego and its desires for the Third-dimension.

All is, and It patiently awaits your focus and desire to be one with It again. Do not attempt to give any project any form or try and create a body concept in your consciousness, but allow the "All" to bathe your dimensional consciousness with Warmth and Light as you experience the "All" within and without your present conscious state. It cannot be captured by any devils or Astral Lords, for they cannot exist in the expansion of Its rays of Light which emanate from Brahman.

Do not seek your higher consciousness within the Illusion that spreads its dark shadow across the Third and part of the Fourth-dimensions, for your higher consciousness does not exist in these perverted frequencies.

Neither should you concern yourself with what others are doing in their spiritual search, for it is not by example that you will gain personal contact with your higher consciousness, but only by being silent and listening to its inner urges and acting on them. Only then will you be able to distinguish between the thoughts flowing from your Ego and those emanating from your higher consciousness. Remember the previous Transmissions' message that there is no actual past or future but only the changing frequencies flowing through your consciousness. Should you "look" back into your past, you are only changing your "view" in consciousness, for when you "remember" something, you are actually experiencing it at that moment.

Many individuals love to read stories on "Time Travel", which express the desire to move backwards and forwards in "time". What does that imply? It shows that many are touching the outer perimeters of their essence, for they sense the reality of being conscious of being ever present in the NOW, wherever it may be, for all IS! And where your consciousness is focused, is where you are in consciousness.

Currently, you are mainly centered within the Third-dimension and that experience is holding your consciousness for a short period of time. It appears to you that you are constantly centered here, and that seems limiting, for you seek to expand the experience by continually dwelling in the Illusion. Your focus on the Third-dimension may last for ten Earth years, or ninety. When you cease to focus on the frequency of this dimension, you are then focussing on another different dimensional frequency. However when you move your dimensional consciousness to be one with your higher consciousness, you are conscious of all frequencies that are flowing through. The closer you are aligned to Brahman, the more you will experience all in all, for there is only one frequency.

What you are doing constantly is allowing your Ego to act as a prism that separates the light into many colors, which distorts the frequency and leads you on the path away from One

Enter the Vortex as One Light

Light and deeper into Illusion.

This present life experience which you are witnessing, as all other life experiences, is purposeful and planned and implemented when your focus is attuned to this dimensional frequency. It will reach its completion in the same way as a composed symphony of music.

Your life has intervals, movements, highs and lows, and your consciousness flows through them as they express the essence and purpose of your higher consciousness until it reaches its predestined completion. You are unaware of its direction and often mistake some of the changes of the rhythms as indicating to you that your life is out of control, for you are unaware of who composed the music and the intent.

Often your life appears to be a mix of uncompleted desires. What you think you want and need is often thwarted, and, in your frustration, you begin to suffer and to blame all outside influences such as governments, friends, nature and God for this misfortune. You are told by the Illusion that you must take charge of your life and raise yourself above such disastrous happenings and then you will not be buffeted by these attacks on your security.

What you do not realize is that it is your "higher consciousness" which composed this music for your experience - its experience. Sometimes the composition is short, or others may be long and demanding. But it cannot be altered until it is played out. There are no pause or stop buttons, for it must continue until it reaches its conclusion.

There is only one composition that your higher consciousness has composed and it is often divided into segments, and is fully played over several life experiences. However you allow your Ego and the Illusion to pervert the flow by interference. This is the karma which is constantly referred to, for the more you interfere with the movement, the more times you must return to allow its completion, and then in one experience you will play the whole symphony completely, and become one with the Third-dimensional frequency.

It is important that you begin to experience the reality of your life now, and attune to the flow of your composition, learn the score and move your consciousness in time with that which is being played. For then you will begin to experience, without pain, all that you composed from your first journey to this Dimension.

You have never been greater than you are now, for all other life experiences have led you to now. Once you move into that frequency of your consciousness which expresses your purpose through your higher consciousness, you will experience the harmony of now. No longer will you be buffeted by disruptive energies, but will follow your experience in a prepared fashion.

It is incorrect to follow the Astral Illusion, which attempts to have you believe that you were sent here to learn the lessons of life and, in the process, suffer indignities and live in fear. You, your Ego, was not sent here. Your higher consciousness moved its face to the Earth and the Third-dimension with one sole purpose and that was, and is, to move the Earth to experience the higher dimensional frequencies of its being. Your Ego has no other commitment than to express that purpose and intention. All other desires and purposes fall within the Astral desire to prevent the ultimate action of the Planet and the Astral loss of control of the Egos.

This is your sole purpose, and the more you attune to your higher consciousness, the more quickly you will get the job done. Align your Ego with the Music of your being, and act in concert together, and move the higher frequencies to the

Enter the Vortex as One Light

Earth.

Remove all desire and feel and listen to those inner urges that are impelling you to the completion of your mission. Align your actions to these urges and you will be experiencing all your Light in the joy of accomplishment, not the personal Ego accomplishment, but the true accomplishment of Brahman in you.

The great elm stands,
defying time
Spreading its glory before Brahman.
Now, it has reached its maturity.
It raises its branches in homage
to its Creator.
It Is!

Annually, it draws its life essence
into the core of its body,
sheds its leaves after a season of fruitfulness,
awaiting its regeneration.

And you,
how long will you maintain
the outward expression of illusion?
When will you stand once more
in all the glory of your being?

Across the heavens,
the eagle soars.
Expression, and freedom in motion.
It rises,
touches the heights of the heavens,
and looks at all below.

It beckons you to aspire to
reach the height of
your consciousness.
To become free - free from all control.

Mankind has forgotten how
to BE.
You are here for the Earth,
just as are all other aspects of Nature.

Move aside from your selfishness,
and bear forth the fruit of your Light.

Feel the Earth,
encourage Light and Love
to flow to the Earth.
Be the Earth.

Grow once more
out of the waters of Life,
and BE where you are NOW!

Understand...
Why you are,
Who you are,
What you are, and
How you are.

Awaken your consciousness,
to BE,
always in the Moment.

From the Vortex.

Transmission
Eighteen

It Ain't Necessarily So!

During your studies of these Transmissions you will find that I have often referred to that frequency of consciousness which has been expressed as "control", and the Astral Lords use this frequency to hold together their Illusion on the Third-dimension, which in turn lulls the Egos of Mankind into a false sense of security and safety. Now is the time for you to tear down the foundations of your Illusion and free the Earth from this perverse domination.

Once you consciously rip apart the Astral structure in your Ego, the Astral Illusion will crumble before your gaze and you will enter into your freedom. Now move your consciousness into the peace of the Vortex and allow the Light of Brahman to illuminate and teach you of the folly of your Ego.

Currently, you are experiencing a heavy overload of control imposed by the Astral Entities on all Mankind, and human beings accept such control as a necessary factor in their lives in order that they may continue to grow in power and wisdom. This acceptance began many thousands of years ago on the Earth. In fact, it began when you first projected your consciousness into the early Earth-bodies. The Ego soon became attached to the illusionary greatness projected to it by the Astral Lords when the Ego existed mainly on the Lower level of the Fourth-dimension. What is not readily understood is that the Astral Lords are unable to have a physical presence on the Third-dimension. As such they use your Ego's frequency on the Fourth-dimension to influence the development of consciousness on the Third-dimension. The frequency of the Illusion has its roots in the Fourth-dimension and is projected through your Ego into the Third-dimension. For the Illusion to be effective on the Third-dimension, it requires the participation of many Egos, and through this cooperation, some Egos have willingly aligned their consciousness with that of the Astral Lords, working constantly in league with them to merge the Astral frequency on both dimensions.

Many consider that the Astral Lords are evil and bad, and behave in a satanic manner. Emotive recognition of good and evil only exists in the Illusion. Whatever you consider as being evil or dark only exists in your consciousness blinded by the Illusion. It does not even exist in the Astral consciousness, for that consciousness is a frequency of Brahman which is not expressive of Egoistic emotions and feelings. The emotions of fear and hatred belong only to the Third-dimension in the Ego frequency, and as such do not occur on any other dimension of Brahman. The Astrals are depending on your Ego to move these frequencies into the Earth's consciousness so that should the Earth be successful in its Ascension, it will take these frequencies with it into the higher levels of the Fourth-dimension and will contaminate the frequencies of that dimension.

It Ain't Necessarily So.

The mechanism by which the Astral Lords formulated the Illusion was through developing specific rules, and these rules are designed to hold Ego consciousness in bondage. Currently, your Ego, and the Earth-body which it uses, works and lives under the domination of thousands of rules. Should you break any one of these rules then you are dealt with in a certain manner.

I spoke earlier of how the Astral Lords, during the sleep stages of the body consciousness, created images of Gods and Goddesses who exerted power and domination over each other and the elements. This was done in order to give credence and power to the many rules abounding in the Illusion. These "divine" authorities soon gained mass acceptance in the inter-connectedness of Mankind's consciousness. What was projected into Man's consciousness during sleep was soon re-enacted in the waking state. This saw the development of the priest cults and the enactments of the Gods became rituals. The cults developed into religions and the rituals became the determination of the behavior of the masses. In some cultures the rituals demanded sacrifice to appease the Gods, and so the Illusion became a strong force on the Third-dimension.

The priests developed great power and control over their people and used the frequency of fear and punishment to hold all within the rules of their Illusion. They then developed the monarchy, kings and queens to represent some of the Astral Gods on the Earth.

Down through the millennia the Illusion grew and became the sole basis for the existence of the life of the Ego on the Earth. You may feel that this could only apply to the primitive mind, but, alas, you are still controlled by your Ego's acceptance and participation in the Illusion.

You live in a totally controlled society, one which constantly regulates all that you <u>do</u> and <u>think.</u> You accept the rules as creating an ordered and peaceful existence for all who inhabit the Earth. You live in fear of transgressing those laws, and if you do, then you will suffer the punishment which is relative to the seriousness of the transgression. And yet, hourly and daily, someone falls foul of this authority which administers the rules and laws of the Illusion. From this, you will understand that not every Ego develops a fear of the Illusionary decrees, but often this lack of fear is due to ignorance and only a few Life experiences.

The Astral Lords and their Entities decided to remove the Gods and developed the concept of "One God", which on one hand was a loving father, and on the other hand was to be feared. Whether the God was loving or severe depended upon just in what manner you behaved. If you obeyed the rules of the Illusion the God was always loving, but if you broke the rules the God would deal out severe punishment. From the God Illusion there developed nearly as many religions as there are people of different nationalities, and each had the same God in namelessness, but it was the savior of their country against the God of their neighbour. So there is one God in name, and different expressions of the same God throughout the different cultures in the World. However, all the religious cults on the Earth have a book of rules to which the members must maintain adherence, otherwise they are punished either physically, emotionally or spiritually.

However, as I previously said, there are always some who rebel, who cannot live under the rules because for they feel that they are free spirits. However these people are usually cast out of the society in which they were born, and are labelled as being "nut cases". This labelling ensures then that they will have little effect on the smooth working of the Illusion.

It Ain't Necessarily So.

Do you feel, in the current expression of your Light, that you are now free from the control of your Ego? It is timely that you assess your relationship with your Ego. You will find that you are still highly regulated by the Illusion. In fact, if you are honest, you will see that your current life experience is dominated by rules which mirror those of the Astral Illusion.

Currently, you are more dominated by your Ego's self imposed rules than are most others living on the planet. I am directing this to you who are studying these Transmissions now, for you have reached that point in your life experiences where you are more controlled by rules than are others.

At some particular point in their many life experiences individuals decide that they have had enough of the materialistic aspect of the Illusion, however they are generally ignorant of the depth of the Illusion and choose to devote their time to following a spiritual path which, they hope, will lead them to peace and enlightenment.

In following such a worthy path, the individual learns that there are certain rules, disciplines and practices which must be adhered to if the desired result is to be attained. It is said that purification of the mind, emotions and sometimes the body, is required in order for one to be freed from the suffering of the Third-dimension.

Where did these rules and practices originate? Many have been gleaned from the writings of those who previously trod the path. Others are taught by Gurus who have the information. There are many secret societies who claim to teach mastery and power over life. Most of these are the outer schools of the Astrals who use them as training grounds for future Entities.

Have you ever questioned what experiences the truly illumined writers moved through in order to attain their enlightenment? You will find that they followed a trodden path of rules and practices until they reached a point where they saw that this was crushing them, and once they said "enough", then and only then, did they move out of the Illusion. All the rules and practices are instigated by the Astrals, for they know that the more rules they place you under, the more you will be kept from breaking free and Being.

Some individuals call themselves "seekers of truth". Constantly they seek whatever will liberate their soul from the bondage of the Third-dimension, for they feel that it is the Earth which holds them captive. They seek it here, there, within and without, and never seem to find IT. They discipline their behavior to such a degree that they constantly await their moment of enlightenment. Do you fit into this category?

Do others look up to you, acknowledging your spirituality? For have not you often expressed that you are no longer interested in worldly fame, and that all your energies are devoted to that of a higher life living in truth! As others sit and hang on your every word, does not this provide some satisfaction to your Ego? Seekers are Ego controlled to a very large extent, although they vehemently negate it. You cannot experience Oneness unless you separate yourself from the rules, especially those rules of your OWN making through your Ego.

Now you have reached the highest point of Astrality, for you can move to become a master in the Illusion - an Entity, or you can turn your back and discover your true essence.

Stop seeking and you will be. Do not search for the truth, for there is no such thing. Truth in the Illusion is a concept that has been Astrally instigated, where all truth lies in how well you understand and live in their Illusion. They use phrases such as, "It is right - it is the Truth"; "When the student is ready the Master will appear"; "Do not doubt the wisdom of the Ages, for it is a test of your faith."

It Ain't Necessarily So.

All religious leaders are Astrally motivated to lull the mass of their followers to accept their rules, to follow those rules and be saved.

Stop seeking and you will be. Do not focus on the future, waiting for it to happen. It is all happening NOW. Live the moment in your consciousness and you will begin to hear and feel the urges of your true essence. Always listen and feel and watch your powerful Ego become a powerless part of your being, unable to pull any more energy from the Illusion. It will blame you for its failure, claiming that you are failing by not listening to it any more.

Once you have made the choice, and move your Ego from the Illusion, you will initially feel that you have nothing. However you cannot now turn back to face the Illusion, for the die has been cast. The rules you sought and followed as a seeker were based on the writings of those who, later, moved out of the Illusion. Now there is nothing written, no guidelines for you to follow, for now you are alone and will experience the alone in the brilliance of the light of Brahman.

You have broken all your personal rules and by doing so you will discover that you were always enlightened. There is nothing to seek, just be the Light and give it freely.

The more you develop rules in your daily activities, the harder you become not only on others but on yourself and the lower your self image becomes. In this instance you certainly are not a free spirit. How can you be free and at the same time live a life which is locked into the rules of the Ego? The Ego constantly refers to this as being "self control".

It is not so much your daily movements - of eating, working and playing etc, which are a problem, but it is the rules which decide how these should be done. You will understand your rule-making when you see how often the results which occur were based on fear existing in the illusionary consciousness of the Ego. Fear is not a part of your inner essence, so this is the guide by which you can understand those actions resulting from Ego influence, and those of your inner Light.

Often you will not acknowledge that your reaction is fear related, rather you attach to your consciousness the feeling that you have broken one of your precious rules for life, survival and power over others. You love your rules so much that you constantly inflict them onto others who possibly have not developed as Astrally as you, and work under less rules than you. Worse still for you is when another's rules conflict with your own, and this leads to the battle of proving just whose rules are right and represent the truth.

Once you are able to expose your rule-ridden Ego, you will find that you are breaking down the Astral Illusion, not only in yourself but also throughout the Third-dimension.

Those who pass out of the Illusion and into their own Light are free to choose their path. They can continue to move more energy to the Earth or they are free to enter other levels of their Dimensional being, for they have then completed their commitment by setting their Ego in place to give the Light of Brahman to the Earth. That is why many of the enlightened of the past are no longer operating on the Third-dimension. However, their life experience opened a vortex whereby Light will continually flow to the Earth.

Most of you who are reading this Transmission have reached a high level of Astrality, although you may deny this. However, if you are following the spiritual path of seeking, then your seeking involves following the rules of the Illusion.

You have been drawn into my Vortex in order that you will be able to penetrate the Illusion and break free of Ego control at a faster rate than by following the old path. My Vortex is unconditional, just as Brahman is unconditional. The Astrals, though, are conditional, and a choice is not acceptable to them. They have no options however, for some fish always escape. The power of this Vortex is drawing many to its center, and that will soon place the Earth back on course to reach its true enlightenment and Ascension. Once you stop following rules you will be free in Brahman. You always choose your path and this you have already done. Your work is done once you leave behind a body and Ego which becomes the pure Ego and body of the Earth.

Should you wish to stay a moment and add more power to the Vortex, you can. You will move back to your original Star System in the Fourth-dimension and from your work on the Third-dimension will develop a Fifth-dimensional essence and continue to live in the consciousness of your moment.

For now, allow your consciousness to feel your inner urges. Be silent, listen and wait. Surrender to your inner Light, and you will begin to experience freedom. Discard all your rules and fears for they do not give you an iron grip control over your destiny as you are often told. Allow others to be and to experience their freedom, for they too must learn to embrace an existence free of all rules and domination.

Enter my Vortex and shed the unrealities, the laws, rules and stress that are attached to living in the Illusion.

Live in this moment and allow the self destruction of the Astral Entities who are attempting to destroy this beautiful Planetary consciousness. In doing so you will destroy ALL Illusion.

Transmission
Nineteen

The Mirror of Creation
and the
Time Line of Destruction

You know there is no such thing as a line. A line is only a continual representation of many dots or small circles, which, being curved in their circumference, cannot follow a straight path. Your line is only straight when viewed by your linear consciousness, and when it is extended beyond your dimensional field of vision, it curves away from you, following a circular path. The Earth is a circular being, and if something is extended across its surface it must move in a curved manner.

When you allow your consciousness to move along the Time Line of the Earth's consciousness, you will flow in a circular movement and you will perceive that you begin to move back to where you start from, for there is no past or future but you exist only where you are in your consciousness.

The Mirror of Creation

In the early Transmissions through the Capsule, I made reference to the Time Loop which was created by the Astral Lords to cloud your understanding and vision into believing that what the mass of humanity is currently experiencing is new and exciting. The present civilisation believes that its science and technology have reached the pinnacle of achievement and evolvement in the recorded history of Mankind - as a progression from a tribal base to a civilisation on the brink of Galactic expansion.

However all of this so called progression is only the Illusion of the Time Loop, for progression only exists in a consciousness that focuses on power and achievement in the Third Dimensional Universe. Being a loop, the Time Loop crosses over itself at a particular point in line with the universal law of energy. As it crosses over and begins to loop back, it is moving, or spiralling, in the opposite direction to that which it previously moved.

All energy follows this pattern, from the protons and electrons in the atom to the magnetic energies of the Earth itself. Even the body which you are projecting to is built on the same principles of energy flow.

Much of which I have revealed in these Transmissions does not harmonise with the materialistic and earth-bound dimensional mind which is so caught in the Illusion that it is closed to all the knowledge that is there to be used. With the Astral Lords it is quite different, for they have never involved their consciousness directly in the Third-dimension and have used this universal knowledge to fuel the energy for their Time Loop, since this energy loop forms the basis for their Illusion. The Illusion follows a cycle of movement from a primitive starting point, reaching a maximum advancement of dimensional matter and moving in a regression back to the beginning once more.

Because of the length of "time" in the consciousness of the Earth Egos, the previous peak is forgotten as Humanity appears to grind its way through many generations, repeating the same impregnated behavior of the Illusion and always expecting to reach a point of power and control over all that it sees and experiences.

This Time Loop is essential to hold together the Illusion, for should many Egos perceive this deception, the Illusion will cease to exist, because in truth it does not! There is nothing here of an Astral nature that can enslave a free soul who, with clear perception and awareness of their own Light, recognizes the Illusion and its Time Loop for what it truly is.

Even now, at the close of this millennium, there is not sufficient consciousness aware of the deception to destroy it forever. However these Transmissions are the catalyst for the coming change. These Transmissions reach deep into the core of all who become exposed to their message. They do not demand allegiance to anyone or anything, for they are the message of freedom for all free beings. There is no organized movement attached to One Light, for All is in each one of you and you need no others or any organization to become free. No one else can give you freedom from oppression and illusion, only you can do this. Your awakening is now at hand. Grasp it!

Being a Time Loop, all within it is predictable, not only to the Astral Lords and their Entities but also for awakened beings such as yourself. Their predictability is their loss, for as I said in that original Transmission, "The dimensional loop, because it operates on the Third-dimension, shortens when it reaches each conclusion, for it must move in cyclic fashion."

Currently, consciousness in the Illusion is moving through a breakdown and destructive phase. This is evidenced by the repetitive mass killing seen over a span of less than a hundred years. Mass killings are more frequent as the movement through the loop is quickening and moving consciousness closer to the turning point of the loop. Within the span of one generation of life experience, these mass murders are constantly occurring, from the mass murders in the concentration camps, to Pol Pot's killing fields, Tianamen Square in China, the mass graves in Bosnia and the African mass murders of men, women and children.

These killings are no accident but are a cold and calculated destruction of bodies perpetuated by the Astral Entities. The Astrals see no wrong in the destruction of the Earth's bodies, and for them there appears no karma either, since they hold themselves beyond retribution in the Third and Fourth-dimensions. They are always living their retribution since they moved away from their Light source in the higher dimensions.

However, what do these mass murders mean in the present moment of consciousness, and more particularly in the Earth Consciousness? For it is actually the Earth which is being attacked and progressively destroyed by these Astrals. This phenomenon cannot be regarded as a "one off" event in the history of Mankind because its purposes and intent are deeply rooted in the Astral Loop and it forms part of the continuance of the loop itself, creating fear and futility in the consciousness on the Earth. It acts as a negative break, one which produces high levels of aggression in those who witness the events, and pushes these observers into further participation in the Illusion. "Revenge" is their cry, and they move their consciousness further from their Light.

You must become aware of just how these Astral deeds affect your consciousness. Do they bring forward feelings of revulsion, anger and all forms of emotional torment? You must

Enter the Vortex as One Light

see how you actually feel about this Astral assault on the Earth and its bodies, and direct your true feelings to the Earth and not at personal suffering.

Those who have personally witnessed the "murder" will know that there were certain life experiences which drew them to that event of consciousness. However the main thrust of the Astrals is to excite and draw forth deep emotions from these individuals who were actually involved or who had friends and relatives involved. The strong emotional energies radiated by this group of consciousness is taken by the Astrals to increase the power and fabric of their Illusion, for they constantly feed off this type of energy. They increase the events in order to gain more frequent shifts of energy from the survivors. They are the mythical vampires who continually suck the life and vitality of the Earth.

You should neither condone nor condemn the actions of the Astrals. Of necessity however, it is important to end their influence on the consciousness of the human Ego, and all your energies must be directed toward opening your consciousness to move **all** energies to the Earth Bodies, for they are the reflection of the Earth's consciousness.

You know that when destruction occurs to one close to you, you will identify with it, because the emotion of others around you will swamp your Ego, forcing your consciousness into the negative polarity of the Astral Illusion. Should you need to experience this as part of your personal karma that is as it is. If not, then do not constantly dwell on the karma of others, but see what it is doing to the Earth. Use this last as your yard-stick and measure where your energies should be moved, for you are now expanding your consciousness to be the Earth's consciousness. How do you want the Earth to feel?

The Mirror of Creation

Mirror of Creation.

Constantly, you are told that you came to the Earth to learn! To experience life! And that whilst you are living this life experience you will perfect "something" - that you will develop a "personality" - something that will add consciousness to the soul or ego which will make you master of all life.

But which life?

In order to attain this mastery of "life", you must be willing to suffer indignities which will eventually allow you to increase in power.

The question that requires answer is, "Why do you need to suffer? And why do you accept the Astral concept that you must <u>evolve</u>?"

Are you not already evolved, for are you not constantly moving your Light to the Earth? Your Ego does not have to evolve, for it only needs to turn to face your Light.

Mankind does not evolve. You cannot evolve, since what is unchangeable cannot change, that which is timeless knows no time. You feel that the body to which you are attached is growing older by the years, however the only way you know this is through your perception of the image reflected to your consciousness. You say, "I feel different", or "I feel older", yet you accept the ageing process of the body as something of yourself which is gradually dying. How often do you ask, "What is <u>it</u> which is observing the changing state of the body?"

The observer is certainly tied to the Ego, however if it becomes more observant of the Ego, just as it appears observant of the body, then it would know that <u>it</u> is <u>not</u> the Ego either.

Once you begin to move your energy in this direction of

225

becoming aware of the grosser parts of your existence you will begin to develop true separation from all illusionary controls, and remember. In your remembrance you will begin to exist. You do not have to change anything, for you are Being.

You do not belong to the time loop of Astrality. All intention becomes clear to your vision. You see the masks of "truth", which are only deceptions. It is the game of life, one which uses pretense to accomplish whatever control is seen as necessary. The killing goes on in the name of truth, justice and God. Animals are slaughtered in the "search" of life as medical science continually maims and destroys them - life organisms - in the quest for a cure for a "human" ailment. Research of this kind is propped up by greed to produce the million dollar "pill" and add to the coffers of the Astral Entities. Clear vision, when cast out into society, reveals the sickness inherent in the Illusion, and more particularly, allows the viewer to see the point within the Time Loop at which humanity now stands.

The loop will soon be broken, for it is being severed by the Earth itself in its consciousness ascending into Light.

If you are ready to help the Earth, then you must clear your consciousness from all which colors the Ego. In a moment of time you can clear all karma, and the first step is to empower your Being and know that you are not here to suffer, or to follow an evolutionary course, nor to master this environment, but to clear your vision and understand that most of the mistakes you have made now and before are those which your Ego declares you have to make, for it is the Astral Illusion which commands this kind of action, feeling and thought. You need not seek any personal Masters, for that leads away once more from your Light.

Gradually you are coming to terms with your body attachment. Now you must come to terms with Ego attachment, and practice detachment from the Illusionary concepts of the Astral, and purposefully reinforce your detachment of the Ego and Body from your inner Light. The theory of detachment plays on the seeker with the notion of attaining freedom - a movement away from the Third-dimension, gaining the bliss of the Fourth-dimension. Such practices of detachment only end in the achievement of "nothingness" - a basic Ego trip - one which relegates the body to be as a statute - mute, lifeless and purposeless.

Stand alone in your Light and perceive your true power, then mirror it through your Ego, reflecting it into the body.

My Light moves through the Vortex of Light and Healing which, like a sword, cuts away all excess growth which covers the path of Light. Expose your consciousness to your flow of Light. Let it cut through the Illusionary dross which grows over your Ego. This dross of the Illusion is only the continual educational system which props up the Illusion. It is designed to lead your thinking and feeling in the direction of deception, a deception of the body, emotions and mind, one which is designed to sway you into doing things which are negative to the flow of life. These educational systems are often considered as being a protection for a "way of life", to prevent a nation from getting out of control.

A house divided against itself will fall, and a people divided provides the scene for wars and killing, which produces tortured and twisted emotions and behavior. The Loop has reached a stage where it is moving into its retrograde stage. To the Astrals it is now a real need to speed up the progression and tip it into the primitive mode where it can nurture more energy from primitive emotion. To do so the Loop must see the current technology destroy itself and, with it, several billion bodies.

This will not happen again, for the Galactic Lords who

rule the Star Systems on the higher dimensions, have decreed that the Earth must and will ascend to the Fourth-dimension and shed the illusion of the Astrals.

Everything which you consider is of truth, or is of spiritual design, is not necessarily so. You must constantly reverse all the old opinions, the trodden paths, all of which are designed to create an illusion of permanence which will hold you in the loop of re-existence.

What does re-existence mean to your consciousness? The majority of individuals find this idea to be a safety net for life. Re-existence is aligned to the body concept of permanence. It fits with the need for a home, whether it be a cardboard box or a mansion, for it fulfils the need for some form of safety and protection from the harshness of Nature, the attacks of others and the fear of death.

Your Ego consciousness, through the Illusion, accepts the need to re-exist again. However the Earth is not moving in the Illusionary Time Loop. It is attached to the energies of the Galaxy, and is moving on a predestined path, just like you, and is not tied to the Astral Illusion. If the Ego becomes less attached to the Earth-body, then it will see that the only need for re-existence is to destroy the Illusion by moving Light and Consciousness to the Earth.

There is a lot of discussion about photons, which will be responsible for providing more Light to the Earth. You could not be aware of the Third-dimension if you were not continually being bathed by photons. The eyes of your body are photon receptors, for if this were not so you would be less aware of the Third-dimension and the Galaxy. You only become aware of your bodily image through the photons striking it and your seeing it reflected in water or in a mirror. You are only aware of other bodies and all other expressions of the Earth as their mass is reflected by photons to your eyes.

The vision of life, the understanding of all that is, requires the movement of photons through your Earthly consciousness. You only "see" with your eyes because there is light which reflects on the photon receptors in the eyes.

To understand the photonic light stream is to understand your own being. The whole essence of existence lies in the way of Light - Brahman - manifesting in the creation, for you have created your own destiny and you exist beyond all dimensions, for you are all dimensions. You are Brahman and you have created this and all Dimensions.

Harken back to what I have told you about the polarity of creation. All is mirrored out of your reflection and is only mirrored through the Light of your Essence - you too are Brahman.

In Brahman there is no beginning or end but only that which Is - that is, non-differentiated existence. <u>You</u> only "exist" in any Dimension through your projection of consciousness, and to do this you require a vehicle or body to mirror that consciousness.

However in the Third-dimension, your vehicle, your Ego, exists in a state of fear - if not a fear of non-existence, then a fear that there may not be another body to mirror its form. With the ending of the Time Loop, if it follows its destructive cycle, then the availability of bodies becomes limited and the Ego is stuck in the Illusion on the Fourth-dimension, unable to give Light or receive it.

There is another way in which your Ego learns to turn away from the Illusion and that is through its interaction with another Ego on the Third-dimension. Through the love for and of another, you may express the desire to continue living with that loved one through the dimensional planes, even after the death of the Earth-body. Often this experience is expressed as "soul mates", and such closeness occurs when Egos who have worked together and separately through many life experiences come together to bring about a change in their consciousness which in turn brings great Light to the Earth and its consciousness. This partnership does not necessarily have to occur between individuals of the opposite sex, for "sex", as such, is not of any consequence in this endeavour.

Aside from this, the continual pairing of male and female body forms is necessary to the balancing of an individual's intellect and feelings. Imbalance is not the special providence of either the male or the female. In a relationship, the beloved of one only sees the reflection of his or her own nature in the other. That is, the desires and life of the lover are reflected in the form and nature of the beloved. This is the mystery of life in the Third-dimension, a continual pairing of individuals during their Earth experience.

It is the Theater on the Dimensional stage, one which plays on for millions of years, the eternal play of the drama of the essence of Light.

I see your problem in understanding what you are now receiving. However, I will open your vision to understand and allow light to move through all that is you, Me and Brahman.

When you express your feeling of love toward another being, animal or plant of this Earth, you are projecting your Light and Essence, and what you receive back to your consciousness is only that which you reflected out in the first instance. However it returns in a different frequency, for it appears that the object which absorbed your outflow is responding. Is it responding or are you responding to your own feelings?

Everything is mirroring something back to your consciousness. What appears to mirror you is also using you as its mirror.

This is the fundamental sequence of the life process, for nothing really exists except your Light and its projection. There is nothing more than Brahman - are you not Brahman?

Take two mirrors. Place one on front of you and the other offset behind you. Stand in front of one of the mirrors. The photons will allow the reflection of your body mass in the mirror which you are facing. You will see the form reflected in the mirror behind you and again reflected smaller in the mirror in front of you. Reflections will continue in both mirrors, getting smaller and smaller as you view them.

You can become lost in these reflections, not knowing which reflects the first image, especially if you are experiencing consciousness in the tenth or hundredth reflection.

You will have forgotten when you first stood in front of the first mirror. This is what self remembrance is. You must remember who the "observer" is, because you constantly feel that the reflection is truly the real you.

Allow yourself to remember - then you will remember Brahman.

Love abounds throughout Brahman.

Transmission Twenty

Of the Moment

Y ou are a moment of time. When I say "moment" I am not expressing a passing of time or an instant experience, for your moment in time now is all that life experience of which you are now aware. It is all one life, one moment within the consciousness frequency of you. This frequency can be understood as being your moment in the Third-dimension, here on the Earth.

When you apprehend what this moment represents to your consciousness, it will become obvious that time is nonexistent. Once you move into the consciousness of your moment, you will experience timelessness, because one, fifty or five hundred years measured by the Illusion on the Third-dimension is just that - an illusion.

When you integrate your Ego and its frequency with the Vortex of Light and Healing, you will sense a separation from the Astral Illusion. All past life experiences will become one life and will be seen as your "moment" in consciousness.

Over the millennium there has been much written and

discussed about "fate", and the fatalistic concept has been instigated by the Astrals to lull individuals into a sense of abandon-
ment - abandoning the need to complete tasks which appear to
be too hard and which involve effort, then assigning all to fate,
such fate as determined by Astral rule.

The concept of fatalism, like many other concepts and
movements in society, has its roots in truth, and fatalism in its
actuality should be seen as representing the predetermined path
of your Light in its work for the creative expression in
Brahman.

Some people often assert that prior to their entering their
current life experience on the Earth, they mapped out and predetermined all that they will accomplish in the oncoming experience on the Earth. Again this is not completely true, for there
is only "one" moment when you predetermined your need on
the Earth and the Third-dimension, and that is when you first
agreed to project your consciousness to the Earth and its Third-
dimension, for there is only one purpose of your life here. And
each return only provides you with the basic need for the completion of your destined path.

The length of the "moment", or the number of experiences, is bound up in just how fixed you become in the Astral
Illusion. There is no time in Brahman, and the return times
become a break in the moment. The time between life experiences appears to increase the moment, but actually it does not
have any effect.

You ask, "What have I predetermined?" This is a common thread of enquiry passing through all humanity, and
expresses memory loss. This memory loss becomes convenient,
for it allows you to move through many transgressions, and all
transgressions are not bad or evil, they are only movements into
the Illusion. However, it is interesting to see that all such trans-

gressions are fraught with suffering, Again, this suffering is not harmful to One Light, for initially these illusionary transgressions are enjoyed and sought after. It is only after the repetitious experiences are seen as fruitless and the cause of much suffering and misery to the Ego, that it seeks to move out of the Illusion. In doing so, the Ego must retrace its old path, and this is accomplished by making amends by reducing the old karma, that is, by ceasing the repetitive transgressions.

At that point in the moment you begin the journey back to remembering what was originally encoded. You begin to toss away the rubbish and excess baggage and move toward the fulfilment of your original purpose.

In the current stage of experience, the Ego sees its "purpose" of life as the becoming of a beacon for all others to follow. Some feel that they should become a humanitarian, a religious leader, a composer of uplifting music, an artist, a teacher, and so the list continues. These Egos feel that through attaining great achievement in these areas they act as examples for others to follow, and this will lead others to find salvation. But salvation from what? A life free from pain and suffering, a life which provides satisfaction, wealth, and all that is considered in the Illusion as being "good". These exemplary Egos act as role models for others, and exert this Astral feeling into the memory of the race, and this is their claim to immortality.

Is that what you consider as being an accomplished and purposeful life?

What is it that you need to remember? What purpose exists beyond all these "purposes" currently entertained by the Ego? What is there which is greater than being a beacon for others to follow?

You are not a beacon, for all others are **you**. When you attempt to influence others, you are only influencing your **self**!

Of the Moment

Your purpose is not to become involved in the lives of others, but to become centered in your own life experience and work it out. It is necessary that you influence your Ego into accepting the flow of your Light into the Dimension. Once you remember **your Self - your Light** - then others will automatically begin to remember themselves. For their Light is also your Light - all is One Light. Once you are One Light you need not try to lecture others about what they should or shouldn't do, for that way exists only in the frequency of the Ego and the Astral Illusion.

Once you remember your true purpose you live in Light and the moment is complete, since Light is flowing through the Dimension to the Earth.

What is the Earth? Most individuals tend to look on the Earth as their private camping ground. The scientific community states that the Earth is an inert sphere of gases and minerals which exists to provide a place for life, especially the human.

Where you now stand in consciousness in the Vortex you must constantly seek to "feel" the body to which you are now projecting. You need to harmonise it to the frequencies of the Earth and to not inflict your Ego's demands on it constantly. You need to know its potential of consciousness, for you hardly pay it any heed, because you never feel that it is separate from your Ego. You need also to separate your Light from the Ego and your Earth-body.

For your meditation and contemplation, try to see what the Earth would be like without the Astral Illusion. You can do this, for there was a time in your consciousness when the Earth did not function within the Astral Illusion.

Once you reach that point in consciousness where you can separate the Earth, the Earth-body, your Ego, the Illusion and You, then you will see and know the Earth in all its glory and purity, the magnificent being which it is. You cannot do

235

this easily while you allow your consciousness, through your Ego, to give power to the Illusion.

It seems difficult for you to divorce your consciousness from the frequency of the Illusion, for you still believe that it exists. I hear you say, "But all civilization on the Earth exists through the Illusion, and to deny the Illusion will deny my existence on the Earth!"

You, or more particularly your Ego, says this, for in that statement you still feel that you exist on the Third-dimension. This is rather than acknowledging that it is your Ego which exists through its Earth connection.

Is there a frequency in consciousness where the Ego will deny the existence of the Illusion? If so, does that mean non existence?

There is no such thing as non existence. The Illusion becomes a reality not to the body, but only to the Ego frequency, and the Ego is the driving force to the body. If this is so, it is also the driving force to the Earth's growing consciousness, for the Earth and its bodies are inseparable.

If the Ego frequency was withdrawn from the body, what would be the experience to the Earth? Can the body exist separately from the Earth? Can the Earth exist separately from the Ego? To both these questions the answer is "yes", with qualification.

The Earth, as the child of the Sun, exists in that frequency relative to the energies and consciousness of the Sun itself.

Now, as the Earth-bodies are a progression of the expanding consciousness of the Earth, then they are capable of separate existence from the Ego. This was the case in the early development of the Earth's consciousness. However, because the Earth needed a higher frequency vehicle to attract higher frequencies of consciousness, the Ego was developed, as a

236

reflection of part of the Sun's energies.

The so-called "vital force", "chi", or any other name attributed to a force which animates the body, exists separately from the Ego, for it is a frequency that is, and has been since the formation of the Earth, continually directed through the Sun throughout the Solar System.

All the Earth, and all that exists in and on the Earth, is bathed with this vital energy frequency, which is the animator of the life consciousness of the Earth. It enlivens all life from the minerals through the plants and vegetation to the animal organisms.

Initially, the developing frequencies in the plants and organisms formed the simple Third-dimensional consciousness of the Earth, and through the process of morphogenesis the organisms became more complex. Such complexity of form and energy allowed the Earth to draw higher frequencies of consciousness to itself.

Before we approach this subject from a deeper level, I want you to move into meditation and during that state begin to sense or feel your Earth-body, for unless you truly feel it and blend with it back into the Total Consciousness of the Earth, you will continually feel attached to the body and will separate its existence from the Earth.

******

The Illusion, and in particular the Ego, makes a strong emotional attachment with the sexual act when performed by the human being. And often the act is separated from its basic function of forming more Earth-bodies. The

Enter The Vortex as One Light

Earth maintains its supply of bodies through the sex function, however within the Astral Illusion the sex function is seen as fulfiling some creative act. It is considered as giving "creation" to the body and its Ego. The Illusion sees this as an elevation of the Ego to replicate the creative action of God. Because the Illusion attempts to elevate human consciousness into comparing it to a God, this allows a feeling of rightness in the Ego to exert a sense of power and domination over the Earth and the Third-dimensional Universe. By assuming this power the Ego allows the Astrals to dominate the feeling frequency, or what is commonly called the feminine nature, whether it is expressed through a male or female body. Domination such as this is one of the major pillars which prop up the Illusion.

Essentially it is true that the act of copulation is an aspect of the creativity of Brahman. In the Third-dimension it is solely for the formation of new vehicles for the expression of life for the Earth. For the Astrals it is an area of further domination and control. For the Fourth-dimension it is the integration of the higher frequencies, that of blending feeling with the intellectual aspect of the Ego, which results in an expansion of Light. Through all dimensions it is the flow of Brahman experiencing its own nature and growth. Once the Ego moves away from the Illusion, then the joining together of Earth-bodies as one allows the God/Goddess energies to flow through all Dimensions, reflecting the Light of Brahman in creation.

However, when an Ego uses the act as a means of domination and control, the flow of Light is cut off at that point.

It is seen here that the Ego exists at the frequency where all change must occur. When you separate the body from your consciousness and allow it to be the Earth, then you can flood it with the Light and Love of your Light Being.

For you to do this requires an Ego which is not Astrally

238

motivated but is fulfiling its service to the Earth, since that is what it was created for.

The Ego exists for the Earth, and there are as many Egos are there are Earth-bodies. Actually these Egos are the Earth's Ego, and they will be the Earth-bodies when the Earth moves into the Fourth-dimensional frequency.

Your Ego must be freed from all Astral frequencies, and you need to rid your consciousness of all fear, for fear is the Illusion, to which all else is added. Do not fear annihilation once you move your Ego outside the Illusion.

Without the Illusion on the Earth, life would have been quite different from what is now experienced. The Illusion moves back through many thousands of years. It moves through a spiral loop which has brought civilization back to that level whereby it appears to be developing technology and power. The Loop is not endless, because the Ego and its expression of consciousness on the Earth cannot exceed the power and technology of the Astrals. They are limited by their Dimension, and so too is the technology expressed through the Illusion limited. Soon it will reach that point where it must retrograde back into a degenerating situation caused by the technology itself. All the technology of the Astrals is tainted toward destruction and control through fear, and this in itself represents its own demise.

So that the Earth can be free of the Astrals and the taint of their Illusion, it needs the elimination of the Astral Lords from the two Dimensions. However, what we are looking at is a frequency, and the Illusion exists at specific frequencies within consciousness. Once the Earth's consciousness moves beyond these frequency bands, the Astrals and their Illusion will cease to exist for the Earth. So it is necessary for the Earth to ascend, and ascend with purified Egos which will represent its vehicle of consciousness on the Fourth-dimension. Only then will your

Enter The Vortex as One Light

Ego truly move beyond the control of the Astrals. However, your Light Body never has, nor will ever be, tainted by the Astrals, for they cannot reach its frequency.

Should there not have been that influx of Astral frequencies to the Earth there would not have been the Illusion and the Earth would have been quite a different place in consciousness. To view life without the Illusion would be to see the Earth's consciousness free from fear and control, selfishness and repressive emotions. Wars and disease would not exist in the Earth-bodies which would be filled with Light.

There would be no greed, and allied to that, no hierarchical systems of control, because all are equal in Brahman. Civilization would still have advanced out of cave-like structures, for consciousness in its pure form would have used the resources of the Earth only for need and not want. All would move progressively toward the Fourth-dimension.

Everything would exist without any Illusion. Many see that money is a product of the Illusion. It is not money which is the problem, rather the intent and greed that flows with its use. Money in itself provides a system of accountability and in itself has no value other than allowing an exchange of service. However the Illusion has made it into a variable reality, a reality which supersedes its value as a system of exchange of service.

Money is seen Astrally as creating a competitive arena for greed, accumulation and control, as it leads the mind of Mankind away from Light and creativity.

Without the Illusion, life would flourish and all work would be an expression of the greater infusion of Light moving through Egos centered toward body feeling. However this did not occur, and the Astral Illusion does exist as a frequency within the realm of the Third-dimension. Being a frequency, it only exists through several layers of consciousness, and as I have previously stated, the Earth will ascend beyond this.

When your Ego ceases to face the Illusion of the Astrals, the Earth will receive the full flow of Light passing through it. The Ego appears to some of you as an enigma, that is, it seems to operate separately from the body and the flow of Light. This is only the illusionary function of the Ego. As was the Earth-body, it was created as an expression for the Third-dimension especially for the Earth, and it is an expression of consciousness through the frequency of the Sun.

You will remember that in the early Transmissions in "One Light", I told you about the radiation belts surrounding the Earth, and how your Light flowed through the Sun and attached itself to a permanent Ego prior to moving through the Life Vortex into the Earth-body. The frequency of the Ego is similar to that of etheric matter or energy. It is a spectrum of energy which is of a faster frequency then the Earth-body, ranging through an energy spectrum from the pre-electron to the first level of the Fourth-dimension. Thus it acts as a connecting link between the lower level of the Fourth-dimension and the frequencies of the Earth and the Third-dimension, and, as such, it holds together in form all the energies of the Third-dimension and in particular the Earth-body.

No wonder the Ego feels that it is the body most of the time, even while, through its connection with the Fourth-dimension, it is able to move the Light essence of your being to the Earth.

Notably, this Fourth-dimension connection of the Ego made it an easy prey for the Astral Lords who have their consciousness in the lower levels of the Fourth-dimension.

In many of the old writings and the fables handed down over millennia, the Ego/Earth-body relationship has been held to be the original expression of consciousness - the frequency of human beings - and the beginning of polarity, for the compatible working of the Ego/Earth-body was the flow of Light to the Earth itself. Consciousness was united as One - One Light expression.

It was only after the Astral Lords gradually drew the Ego toward the Illusion that the separation occurred and the Earth and its consciousness - its bodies, experienced a separation and suffering by being denied Light and purpose. In all simplicity this is what happened and why you now experience that separation in your anguish. It was that moment of separation which represents your "moment" of a continual struggle to break free, to be what you always are, and these Transmissions are awakening you to that which you have forgotten.

In the Earth year of 1995, the Vortex of Light and Healing was moved through the Sun to the Earth, and it is the Vortex of Prime Energy radiating purposeful Healing and Light to all the Earth frequencies. This Book of Transmissions as given to you, Jon, is also flowing through the energy fields of the Vortex, for they are available to all. Even those who never read your transcriptions will, on attunement, understand this message.

Understand that the Dimensions do not exist separately from each other. When you stand and view the night sky in awe of its vastness and distance, often you imagine that it leads to the Fourth or Fifth-dimensions. Because of such vastness most feel that it is through the Galaxies that all is.

Actually, the Fourth dimension exists where you are now, as well, and so on. It is all frequency, and frequency is a matter of speed and velocity. A simple example of this can be seen when you spin a wheel with spokes. As the speed increases by rotating the wheel faster, the spokes seem to disappear. Should you spin the wheel faster still it too will disappear to

Of the Moment

your vision.

If you did not know that this wheel was there in the first place you would not think that it even existed. However if you walked into it, you would sustain injury but be unaware of why.

The Fourth-dimension exists where you are, but it is moving on a frequency so fast that your dense body moves through it and does not experience any sensation of it. However should you increase your sensitivity, you begin to "see" some of it and take it into your experience. You call those individuals who "see" the Fourth-dimension, "sensitives" or "psychics". However, even such increased sensitivity and expansion of the normal Third-dimensional sense receptors does not make these individuals any more important than others on the planet, for their sensitivity is only an extension of the normal sensual awareness. What is not usually known is that "sensitives" also see many of the degenerative beings and aspects of the lower Fourth-dimensional realm, and this often drives them into a negation of what they sense. One does not express more Light just through observation of what is hidden to the Earth-body senses. Frequently this extra "sight" becomes a distraction, and distraction becomes a major obstruction on the journey of remembrance.

It is important that you experience the "moment" at that frequency which moves your Light to harmonise with your current work, for only in this way will you bring Light into this Dimension.

You do not need to "see" the Fourth-dimension to experience its frequency or to accomplish your purpose, for as your consciousness expands to encompass a wider band of frequencies, you constantly receive more Light through a greater spectrum of dimension.

You are required only to remember yourself, and to

allow others to move their energy towards the same end. Once you become "One Light" you will, of necessity, pour Light to the Earth consciousness, which includes the Earth-bodies of others. The quickening, once started, will never end, and the Illusion will remain, chained to a small band of frequencies of consciousness. Once the Earth moves into those higher frequencies beyond the Astral Illusion, the Earth, and those Egos which move with it, will cease to be aware or influenced by the Illusion. Its destruction will be of its own making, as it will no longer be able to vampire the energies of the Earth and its consciousness. For, as the Earth is no longer anchored in these frequencies, it will begin to birth its own child, and this sickness of Astral Illusion will not influence the growth of the Earth Child. The Illusion of the past will have no effect on the child, for there will be no karma here. All karma of the Earth will be set aside with its ascension.

The Earth existed prior to the Astral descent and the subsequent Illusion, and the Astral involvement is part of the growth and karma of the Earth and its Egos. The memory of how the Astral Lords used this Illusion with the Earth/ Ego/ Earth-body, and how the Earth moved away from the Illusion, is an experience which will not taint the new Earth Child.

These Transmissions have been implanted in the Vortex as energy nodes which align with the energy nodes of your Etheric and Fourth-dimensional bodies. Your etheric body has major and minor chakra vortices as well as many transformer nodes which complete the frequency pattern of your dimensional consciousness.

These Transmission frequencies are flowing through the Vortex of Light and Healing into its moment in the Third-dimension. You can access these frequencies by moving your consciousness through the Third-dimensional pyramid and allowing your consciousness to flow with the ever widening spiral of energy back through the Sun of this Solar System. As you move your consciousness through the Sun and into the Fourth-dimension, you will experience an upliftment and a reversal of polarity - that of the Fourth-dimension, which will move your consciousness back through the pyramid to your Earth-body. This higher frequency will transform all the chakras and nodes, awakening the memory of your true purpose for the Earth.

Once this expansion occurs in your consciousness, you will bypass the Illusion and move your Light through the frequencies of the Vortex into the total dimension of the Earth's consciousness. This will, in turn, draw other Egos toward these frequencies and move them upwards through the spiralling energies of the Vortex, increasing its power and enlightenment for the Earth.

These Transmissions are calling all of you toward the Vortex center, and even those who do not read these words will be drawn into the centre through your increasing its power and energy to the Earth and the billions of body consciousness. The Vortex is now open, and nothing of Astral intent can stop its expanding power and flow. For, as your Light flows back to the Earth, it will enliven the crystalline inner core and the multitude of reflections will light up the planet. The Earth will Shine, not with a glow reflected from the Light of Mother Sun, but from its own inner glow, as it is now ascending in its own Light, reflecting the power of Brahman.

Transmission
Twenty One

One Way

For many thousands of years now, the "holy" men of this Third-dimension sought sanctuary from the world by going into a wilderness, a mountain cave, a retreat or a monastery, on the pretext that they could communicate with God. The messages which they brought back were often tainted by Astral concepts as, in most instances, the God which they drew close to was only the Astral created God.

In Mankind most of the desire to escape lies in a vain attempt to run away from life, a life imprisoned in the Astral Illusion. There is no need to try to escape from this Illusion, for by standing where you are, your consciousness will reveal to you how the Illusion dominates your Ego. The Illusion bases its control on fear, as fear is deeply rooted in the Ego through its long period of attachment with the Illusion. The Earth-body also has been subjected continually to the "fear" frequency and reacts simultaneously with the Ego when you move into fear.

Observe how the Astral Entities consistently use that deep-rooted frequency of fear in consciousness as a means of having your Ego do what they want.

The Astral Entities have, for thousands of years, practiced the use of fear to control the masses under their charge. This was how the ancient priesthood held people in submission. Often this was accomplished by their direct contact with the Gods, and also by sacrificing people in that cause. Once the process of sacrifice was ended, they used the concept of heaven and hell to maintain the fear in their people.

When much of the power of the churches moved to the Government, the same principle was used to hold the population under control. They use fear of war, loss of employment, the spread of disease and many other ploys to keep the individual bonded to their principles. The greatest institution for maintaining fear over individuals is the prison system. Should you break their rules, you are hounded and put into jail and you lose your "freedom", or what is described as "freedom" in the Illusion. Other ways of Astrality are to strip an individual of all their wealth, or in some cases they will remove an individual's children from their care.

The Illusion runs the Earth on the frequency of fear, and fear alone. Dictators use fear to create wars, and elected governments also use fear to wage wars in the pretext that they are protecting the rights of their citizens. Advertising also often uses fear to promote sales of goods and products.

As long as you allow yourself to move into fear you are trapped in the Illusion. When you use fear to control the actions of your family, friends, employees and others you come into contact with, you are increasing your commitment in the

Enter the Vortex as One Light

Illusion.

Medical professionals use fear to bind their patients to them, since their patients fear that without the authority and knowledge of these professionals, they are doomed to illness and death. In fact you will find that all professionals use this frequency as a matter of control over their clients. You cannot help but see that the world runs on fear.

But isolating yourself from the Illusion in retreats is not the answer. Isolation usually means a life spent in yearning, prayer and sanctuary, as such isolation does not produce any power over self. Those who enter Monasteries constantly perform rituals which intensify the power of the Astral God, one which only exists through the energy assigned to it by the followers and aspirants.

Should you remove yourself temporarily from the congested aridity of the Illusion in order to open your heart and mind to just being a Being of Light, then that is a worthy approach. However, once you become Light-expressive and return to the world and its Illusion, you must let your Light shine. You are required to Be where you are, for you cannot be anywhere else. Do not continue to run away from your fears for they do not exist; they are illusionary.

Nowadays you will meet and hear of people who are called "workaholics". Many individuals work constantly up to twenty hours a day, seven days a week. Some people consider that these workaholics must be highly motivated while others consider them to be foolish, missing all the "good things" of life.

What most people do not understand is that these workaholics are living in constant fear of having to face the reality of themselves. When they are working they attempt to shut out what needs to be faced in their consciousness. Often

248

they are running away from a problem of their childhood, or in other cases it can be some karmic experience from a past life. If and when they confront this, they will open their heart and mind to the full Light expression of their being and will cease destroying their bodies.

Look deeply into yourself and face your fears. Expose them to the Light of your Being and you will see that they are truly illusionary, and, as such, have no substance in controlling your actions and feelings.

That is the reason you must "be where you are" and allow your Light to be expressed through your creativeness, and not be dulled by fear, hate and gossip and attempts to rule the lives of others. With your creativeness you can express unconditional love in your life experience. There is no need to go and teach and preach at others ,for there are certainly enough preachers and teachers in the Illusion. Just allow your Light to lead you.

There is no need to follow the old way - that is the way of the Illusion. The current frequency, which has been termed "The New Age", is dedicated to having personal teachers and masters as well as masters and super beings enlightening the Earth Egos from distant parts of the Galaxy. In the initial unfoldment of the Age there was a flow of teachers from many cults in India and Asia. These holy men found it easy to influence lost and jaded, cash-rich Western seekers to follow their path to Nirvana and, in the process, relieve them of their cash.

I emphasized the word men, for it is from men that much of the Astral control stems. Very few women fit the Astral pattern of being a Messiah. However, on occasion, some may, when the Astrals consider it profitable to have an Entity take on a feminine Earth-body. At such times, this occurs in order to wield greater control over the feminine nature of Man and also to generate hope and expectation in the suppressed feminine polarity of the Earth. But the Astrals promote their power grip mainly by maintaining Male polarity dominance, for this creates strength in the pillars of their Illusion.

Often at times in your experience, such as now, you need isolation from the turbulent stress of the Illusion, which constantly pulls you into the negative spirals of frequency that distract you from the degree of work required to move into these Transmissions. This present movement to a place of peace and isolation is not to be viewed as an attempt to escape, because it is temporary - for a purpose.

As you have seen and read from these Transmissions, you are able now to recognize the varying controls surrounding you within the Illusion. Now you are beginning to free your Ego from participation, and in doing so you are beginning to experience freedom.

When the Astral Lords and their Entities find that one is awakening others to their evil ways, they constantly attempt to destroy that individual. However they find it impossible, as they cannot stand in front of the emerging Light of that Being. This occurred when you were attacked by Razparil, Jon, however you had exposed your consciousness to greater intensities of Light, so that you were able to bond your Ego consciousness with Sizzond and, in turn, allow Sizzond to link Light and consciousness through three dimensions. The same applies to all who follow this path now opened. The Vortex is a doorway to Light and is open to all who want to awaken their inner desires. Often the desire is there, but the only route has been through the mine-field of Astral cults, societies and secret orders. Along the way, much of the energies of the seekers is vampired by the Masters and Elders. They attempt to make the seeker dependent for enlightenment upon their false power, and these Astral

One Way

Fakers use these seekers to increase their power in the world of Mankind.

Often, many seekers become jaded with these societies and cults and sever their contact with them. They are unaware though that, having been indoctrinated into the rituals and meditations, they have bound themselves to these Astrally motivated beings and are still working for the purposes of the Astrals and the Illusion.

Individuals who have taken this path become the unwitting puppets of the Astrals - the unconscious Entities of the Astrals who continue to parrot the control measures of the Illusion.

Should you have had contact with any cults and societies and have physically severed your connection, it is important that you break the psychic link. To do so you should gather together all paraphernalia and written rituals and place them in the center of a circle of salt and burn them. This way, and through affirmation at the time of the burning, you will sever all contact with the past and claim your freedom.

The Vortex and these Transmissions will touch many desires and the yearnings inherent in all Egos who are sincerely seeking, for these individuals now stand on the razor's edge. They have come a long way in personal power and can move to either side of the blade. They have trodden the path of the Astrals and did not attain the enlightenment they hoped would follow, for there is no salvation or enlightenment in the Illusion. They must follow a narrow path through all the deception and power that is thrust at them and choose the way of Light, the Light of their own Being.

The opening of the Vortex is widening and the way is clear. For you who have travelled far, the Light is beckoning you to cast aside all illusion from your Ego, for you have known for many lives that there was a way. The Vortex beckons you to move. It is your personal journey. A journey home. There are no obstacles in the Vortex, no conditions, no price. It is free, just as is the Light of Brahman, which flows through all dimensions. Have confidence and move forward to your Light.

The Astral involvement is found in all areas of life and no less than in all the established religions on the planet. Most of the current religious cults in most countries hold to the principle of One God. That is, they claim not to serve any others. In some cases this God is Nameless, whilst in others it is ascribed a name. However you will find that this One God works solely for the needs of the particular religious group. All the One Gods help their adherents to wage wars against others who support another One God. These Gods are asked to protect the faithful, bless particular countries and save people from the tragedies of Nature. In fact, you will find that the adherents of a religious cult in one country often view their God as different to a similar faith in an adjoining country. Sometimes the God is loving and at other times it is punishing. What you see in the world today is no different from the so-called pagan religions of yester-year, that of multiple Astral- dominated Gods all serving the purposes of the Astrals.

It is mostly only when priests move up in the hierarchical chain of a religious organization that they become tainted Astrally. However they are not coaxed to become that way. They want to, for they have been drawn to this type of organization as it is another step toward the Astral power which began in previous life-experiences and still demands fulfilment.

For those individuals who belong to the various religions, they are often ready to move out of that situation into Light because actually they were drawn to the religion through seeking some relationship with a higher being, and quite often they became involved with that mode of worship because their parents belonged to it. Through their involvement, they frequently see the shallowness of the rituals which are constantly moving with the Astral Illusion. Some of these religions have degenerated into becoming "modern", and have cast aside their former rituals which were Astrally motivated, and are basically just areas of social involvement, and of little purpose for the Astrals.

There are no barriers to movement into the Vortex. What is necessary is that those who are seeking their Light should no longer flounder, moving along false paths. For the direct way is One. Do not be fooled by the Astral saying that all paths are one, as that is not so.

Of particular importance is the oncoming frequency of change. It is calling all to it, for it is of higher energies than any ever experienced in this planet's consciousness before. Everything in the last four thousand years has been moving toward this Earth Ascension. There is no need for groups, societies, religious cults, since it is within the individual that the Earth is awakened. All the true enlightened beings who have shone their Light through the Earth proceeded internally and alone in their unfoldment. See this, and know that this is the way for you and all others.

If you wish to, read the many numbers of books published monthly, and discern where Astral concepts are propounded. There are very few works which are free of Astral taints. Once you open your Ego to receive the Light of your Being, you will no longer require books; for you, Light will guide you in truth and knowledge.

Once all systems desirous of leading seekers towards the truth become centered around an individual, and groups form about this individual, it is not long before the Astrals infiltrate

Enter the Vortex as One Light

the group and begin leading it into the Illusion where it becomes a system of hollow words rather than direct feeling.

The Astrals work on words rather than feelings, for they have no concept of feeling. Feeling is the essence of your Light Being, for feeling expresses the Love frequency of Brahman. The Astrals have no love. They exist through the use of greed, selfishness, power and lust. This is certainly not the path of Love.

I am sure you understand now why there will be no Third-dimensional organization built up around these Transmissions, and no single individual to be focused upon as a center, for there is to be no Astral involvement for those on this journey. However, never feel alone in your work. As you move forward in the Vortex we will be as one in Brahman.

Transmission
Twenty Two

Deception

It can only be stated that "Consciousness Exists". The same consciousness moves through all the Star Systems of this Galaxy, this Universe and all other Universes and their Dimensional planes, for it is only the ever expanding consciousness of Brahman.

Human Beings have habitually named everything in their consciousness, beginning with themselves, and they continually invent names for all their discoveries in Nature and the Universe. The small specks of light seen in the heavens have all been named by Mankind and usually correspond to something already named on the Earth, sometimes after the discoverer of the thing. Various stars and star systems in this Galaxy have been named Sirius, Pleiades, etc. Such naming does not create any power since the names only reflect some aspirations and fears held within the consciousness of the Earth-bodies with their participation in the Astral Illusion. However, any Beings

Enter the Vortex as One Light

of consciousness who may flow through the many Star Systems would not claim to be Sirians etc., for they have no relationship with the Earth Beings.

There have been a number of individuals who have sought to contact consciousness beyond the Earth. Not by using space craft or radio frequencies, but through psychic contact or visitation. Late in the Nineteenth and early Twentieth Centuries most of this contact was being made with entities "living" on planets in this solar system, but as science began to develop craft which could scan these close planets, the contacts moved into the Galaxy, far removed from exploration by Earth science.

Consciousness does exist throughout the Galaxy, and on all dimensions as well. When sensitive individuals receive information from Pleiades or Sirius or any other Star or System, why do these "higher contacts" claim to come from systems using the Earth names? In all their greatness they should declare the true name of their system and allow the constant naming process of human beings to be corrected.

There has resulted from this contact with other Star Systems, a constant focus on paranormal experiences. At present there are high expectations of more visitations and the visitors are a blend of aggressive beings intent on destroying the Earth after destroying their own planet, and beneficent beings who will come to the aid of the human race and repel the invaders. To some this conflict heralds the "second coming", while others consider that the alien beings will merge with the current human beings and create some new "super" being.

The consciousness of Mankind is constantly being seeded with these expectations. Who or what is doing the seeding? It is time to address this situation in order that your expanding consciousness will not be deceived any longer, and held in bondage with false expectation.

Deception

The frequencies moving through the various Stars of this Galaxy do not correspond with the Earth frequencies, rather they are aligned with the Sun, and many reach the Earth in the same way that your energies and consciousness pass through the Sun in stages to the Ego and Earth.

These are Light frequencies, and it depends upon their frequency pattern as to how they will affect the consciousness on and of the Earth. All energy which reaches the Earth from the Galaxy and the Universe has a determining effect on the consciousness of the Earth. Much of the Light energy which is currently being received by the Earth moved through the ethers many thousands of years ago, Earth time.

As you learned in these Transmissions, the Earth-bodies have constantly been seeded by consciousness flowing from the various Star Systems through the Sun to the Earth consciousness.

The consciousness radiating from the different Egos on this planet consists of that from other Star Systems in this Galaxy. You are the Sirians, Pleiadians and all other energies from the Stars of this Galaxy.

What then is occurring with the "visitations" of reported aliens who are making deals with different Governments - the Reptilians, the Greys and others who abduct humans?

Always in your thinking and feeling relate what you want to understand to how it fits in with the Illusion, for visitations and other occurrences are imbedded in the Illusion and are being manipulated by the Astral Entities.

The consciousness of Humankind is so entwined with its Earth-bodies that everything is measured relative to the Earth-body and the Dimensional state where it functions. Most individuals find it impossible to distinguish their Ego from their Earth-body, let alone their Light-body from their Earth-body.

Enter the Vortex as One Light

They see in their consciousness, mainly from reading and discussion amongst each other, alien beings visiting the Earth from other Star Systems. The aliens come in ships, which are designed and made in forms recognizable to Earth-beings, usually being saucer-shaped or cigar-like. They are made from elements consistent with or similar to Earth elements. In other words, they have Third-dimensional form, and have windows in order that those in the craft can see out as well as that those on the planet can see in.

Often these visitors are not friendly and they kill animals, abduct humans, keep them for some time and send them back to the planet from whence they came. Such aliens always have recognizable forms with similarities to the Earth-body.

For alien ships to move through the Earth's atmosphere they must be of the Third-dimension. In other words they manifest at that frequency required for Third-dimensional orientation. This being the case they would have to come from a planet which has a similar atmosphere and density to the Earth.

In recent years the Earth governments have developed "inner" space programs, that is, no further from Earth than its moon, whereby they have sent astronauts into space for periods of time ranging over several months. It has evidenced that once the Earth-body is removed from the energies of the Earth - those energies which the body requires for its continued function - permanent degeneration to the body occurs. Long periods of disconnection from the planet will lead to a total breakdown of the Earth-body, as that body is part of the Earth itself.

If alien visitors are also Third-dimensional beings, then they are oriented with the planet which supplied that body. As such, they too could not exist for prolonged periods of time in an environment removed from their energy source.

You ask just what is occurring with these repeated sightings and visitations? There is no doubt that many individuals are having unexplained experiences which are building toward a finale.

Such a finale has a predetermined end, which is given clearly in the message constantly being promoted on the planet. "You have destroyed the environment of the planet, and, as prophesied, a Savior will come and create a heaven on the Earth".

The seeds of this were first sown in the writings of the Apocalypse, which created certain expectations in consciousness for nearly two thousand years.

The real holocaust was meant to be nuclear destruction by the superpowers on the Earth. This was averted in the nineteen eighties when there was a shift in the planetary consciousness, so now the Astral Lords and their Entities are centering the consciousness of the Egos towards an alien invasion, under the pretext that it will unite Mankind. In the initial stage there would be the invasion, and then saving by the friendly aliens. These beneficent aliens will set up government on Earth and guide people in living under their system, which would be seen as being better than the one currently existing on the Earth.

This will give the Astrals total control and more power to the Illusion. Most alien visitations only appear to occur on Earth or in a Third-dimensional atmosphere. As you study and understand your consciousness, you will realize that it is difficult to distinguish between an actual, tangible "conscious" experience and one on the level of consciousness in your Ego. Whatever the experience, it is real, because if the Ego experiences a paranormal event, it will add dimension to it in the same way as in a nightly dream state. The Astral Lords always move your consciousness through "dream-like" experiences, as they cannot function themselves on the Third-dimension. They leave the "hands-on" experiences to their Entities on the Third-dimension.

The alien movement is real in consciousness but is not necessarily a Third-dimensional experience. Look further at what is occurring. At the moment there is a seeding in the consciousness of many of the American Indian nations. They are having visitations in their Sweat Lodges, and individuals, when low in energy or sick, are being exposed to paranormal experiences. This has been popularly reported in the many recent publications of the Earth media which deal with "New Age" information.

The present contamination of the consciousness of the American Indian Nations heralds the last chapter of the current time, for these races have withstood much of the Astral influence that swept Europe and the white North American nations for some thousand years or more. Should the Astrals succeed with their move to control the consciousness of the American Indian Nations, they will move the consciousness of the Egos into a predetermined depth in the Illusion whereby they will unleash their fury for the coming millennium.

The higher consciousness of the Star Systems flows constantly to the Earth, creating that change which will regenerate the Earth, allowing it to move free from the Astral Illusion and end that dominance forever.

You must be fully aware of the constant attempts of the Astrals to use the energy flowing through the Egos for their nefarious purposes, that of breaking from their prison. They will use all manner of deception to accomplish their ends.

Continue to study these Transmissions for they will free you from all deception and all fear, and will leave in their place, Love and Freedom.

*

Deception

You will have seen that I have constantly referred back to your need to separate your consciousness from the Earth-body. It does become one of the major shifts to consciousness in relation to your understanding of the Illusion, as well as of the Vortex and your Light-body.

Your Ego is so related to your Earth-body that it is difficult in most cases to distinguish between what is affecting your consciousness at any particular time. The body is older than your Ego, for the Ego was a later development than the body. There has been no evolution on this Planet, just change, and change occurs as there are shifts in consciousness. As the consciousness of the Earth shifts to the Fourth-dimension, changes will occur on a Dimensional level as well.

The remains of human and human-like Earth-bodies have been recorded as having existed for millions of years. The Ego has been engaged with the Earth-bodies for many hundreds of thousands of years. During that period there have been a mixing of functions which eventually have been considered as one. This is causing difficulty to each one of you as you attempt to be conscious of your Light-body.

Early in the development of the Earth-bodies, consciousness was centered in the functions of the body. Such consciousness involved movement, expression, communication through different sounds, and energies which stimulated the appetite, as well as those glandular secretions which moved the Earth emotions at that time.

The Earth-bodies moved through the process of regeneration through sexual intercourse between the male and the female polarities. The inherent consciousness was moved through the cells progressively by the sexual act, for once a body terminated, it moved back to the elements of the earth, and all consciousness and remembrance of that body ceased. All consciousness of the Earth-body moves in the continuum of the DNA in the prime cells. This caused a development of a Matrix of consciousness which moves through the generations of bodies. Even today, in families, it is often stated by some observers that one child seems to act and behave much like the father or mother. The consciousness of the body is wrapped in this flow and is the power for the continual rebuilding of the body. It is powered by the interaction of the energies of the Sun in conjunction with the Earth.

The Ego, on the other hand, has its roots of consciousness on the lower levels of the Fourth-dimension. Its energies are not powered by the Sun, which consists mainly of Etheric frequencies of the highest level of the Third-dimension, but by the energies of the Fifth-dimension and the Light field of consciousness.

The Ego expresses emotion and mind functions on a different frequency than the body. However it is integrally connected now to the Earth-body. The major problem which you are currently experiencing is that of feeling bodily attached and centering consciousness on the Fourth-dimension. In other words, you do not actually feel centered in consciousness in the body, but about and outside it. However you find it extremely difficult to be Fourth-dimensionally oriented and ground your feelings on the Third-dimension.

The next step in your understanding is to know that you need to become a Light being, or a being centered on the Fifth-dimension. You find it difficult enough to be a being centered on the Fourth-dimension and deal with the Third-dimensional consciousness of the body simultaneously. When you move to the consciousness of your Higher dimensional self, you will then need to become a being centered with consciousness on the

Deception

Fifth-dimension and be conscious on the Fourth-dimension and grounded on the Third-dimension. That is not a problem, for that is what consciousness is. However, for you to unleash the power of your Higher being, you must first harmonize your relationship of the Third and Fourth-dimensional awareness - NOW. Once this occurs you will move your center of consciousness to the next dimension.

Meditate on this because it is a major key for your movement into consciousness. You will readily see the Vortex and we will be as one in the Vortex, and the Earth will rise with all of us.

In Peace and Love, I leave you to study and grow, for once you begin to move, I will send more Transmissions to assist your movement into total Light and Brahman.

The Finale

The last two and a half years have seen, for us, unthought of changes to our consciousness. The living of an experience in some ways becomes alive more on reflection. The discovery meant a lot for both of us. We lost Carl along the way but were aware that his passing was his freedom. The message was given in "One Light" to those seeking the truth and freedom from the Astral grip on the beautiful consciousness flowing through humankind and the Earth.

It is still only the beginning, as the moment is eternal in Brahman.

I know that many have been awaiting the publication of these Transmissions and at last we are able to send them out to the Publisher knowing that they will face a tremendous amount of work in the editing and preparation.

After having found harmony with "One Light", many have written to us over the last ten months, telling of their personal experience with the message. I have not answered anyone personally for we were busy with the Transmissions, and I also felt, in keeping with the purpose of Zadore, that each one of us must bond in the Vortex. Rather than create a personal dialog, it is better that you move your energies to the Vortex and It will produce that freedom which only experience can supply. That is more than words can accomplish.

We know that you will experience an accelerated move forward in your Light and consciousness as you take these Transmissions into your consciousness as a living experience.

Finale

Every day you will experience that break from the Astral Illusion which has much control over your Ego.

Recently we journeyed to the Vortex here in the Third-dimension where Zadore moved its energies into the crystalline patterns of the Earth itself in November 1995.

We stood in silence, alone but for the sea birds and the gentle caressing breezes of the Pacific Ocean.

We stood there, before that natural pyramid, experiencing the energy patterns which continually pass through the multi-dimensional planes, now manifesting and grounded on the Third-dimension.

Our bodies seemed to mold into the Earth energies flowing through the many chakras which link our consciousness with the Earth-body and the Earth itself.

A Moment, as you know, lasts forever. So moments such as this are endless in consciousness. For how often do we re-experience such moments?

Our bodies and your body are linked to the energies of the Vortex through the ever expanding energies of the Earth.

So we are not alone, for the Vortex links our consciousness with all others walking the Earth. We know that the Earth will be safe from all the intimidating frequencies. That there will be a fusion of energies and that the Ascension will rise from the dross and ashes of the battle.

We also know that there will be much for us and for you to do, for as we move our consciousness to the higher frequencies of the Vortex, our perception will be expanded to see more clearly what is occurring, and the intent of the Astral Lords and their Entities.

Remember not to move into fear, but always expose the fear with white light. When you falter or fail do not lament, but move on and focus on the Light and Brahman.

Enter the Vortex as One Light

Do not put Earth-Illusion dates on when certain events may or may not occur; the Earth-Illusion calendar is not accurate. Prophesy belongs with the Illusion. What the mass expect may happen to them if they believe it to be, however it is unnecessary for you to create outcomes in the Illusion. Focus on your freedom and you will be sure that the Earth too will be free.

Soon you will be advised when the Journey Oracle Cards will be available. You will be able to use them to stimulate your higher feelings as you journey through the Vortex.

For the moment, we will enter into the energies of the Vortex and will be with you all on the way to One Light.

Jon Whistler.

266

Glossary.

Astral:

The Astral is commonly thought of as being connected with the stars. It is also another term for the Fourth-dimension, and it describes a level of frequencies found between the Third and Fifth Dimensions. The lowest band of frequencies of the Fourth-dimension is located between the radiation belts and the Earth. It is that atmosphere which the Astral Lords and their Entities inhabit.

All the planets in the Universe have astral frequencies surrounding them, consisting of pure energy that acts as an environment for consciousness passing into and out of the Third-dimension.

Astral Entities:

Those many individuals working in various positions in government, military, monetary and other authoritarian areas of the world who have turned away from their Inner Light and aligned their consciousness with the Astral Lords for the purpose of maintaining the Illusion and its control over Human consciousness. In the aspiration to become as the Astral Lords themselves, they follow the agenda of working for the control and destruction of the Earth and its inhabitants. They are driven by greed and dominance.

Astral Illusion:

The Illusion is like a veil over Human consciousness which distorts reality and distracts the Ego from being One in the Light of Brahman, and is the creation of the Astral Lords. By holding individual consciousness in this Illusion, the Astral Lords are able to draw energy continually from the Egos in order to perpetuate their illusionary environment. This energy which they draw is energy meant for the Earth and its consciousness.

Astral Lords:

These are beings who, at one time, dwelt in the highest Dimensions of Brahman, and because of manipulation and greed, expelled themselves from the Light of these Dimensions. They were imprisoned by the Galactic Lords in the Fourth-dimensional atmosphere which exists close to the radiation belts of the Earth. They cannot make physical contact with the Third-dimension and rely upon influencing individuals of that dimension while those individuals are in the dream state. Also they rely upon the assistance of the Entities who have aligned themselves with the Astral agenda.

Astral Time-loop:

To maintain a belief in the "progress of civilization", the Astral Lords created a time loop within the Illusion. Being a loop, Time must always return to its beginning, after a period of "growth". Each movement through the loop erases the memory patterns of the previous time-loop, so that Human consciousness believes that it is inventive and is expanding new knowledge. However there is nothing new in the time-loop, since all has occurred before and has only been forgotten. What seems "new" is merely a re-discovery. However, due to the powerful memory patterns inherent in the Earth, the memory of previous epochs cannot be suppressed altogether and once this re-awakens in the Human consciousness, it becomes necessary for the Illusion to speed up the progression towards destruction of the learned technology.

Brahman:

There is no such being as Brahman. Zadore uses this term to express the Ever-creative Light of the Universe. All that is in all universes of all dimensions are of this Brahman Light. It has no name, but the word Brahman is used only to avoid using the word God, as it would relate to the "God" concept of the religionists.

Brahman is Light and holds no personal contact with any individual, for all is this Light and is not separate, from a grain of sand on the beach to the mountain range above it, from the consciousness within you to the consciousness of the stars.

Chakras:

An Eastern term relating to the energy "flowers" which connect the Etheric energies with the physical form, and the Astral energies with the Etheric form. There are major chakras which connect with the endocrine glands in the body plus many more which are found at the body's acupuncture points, as seen in the charts detailed in Chinese healing. The chakras are basically vortices which allow consciousness and Light to flow into the Third-dimension, and vice versa.

Earth-body:

The physical body. Unfortunately, due to the Illusion, most individuals believe and feel that the body is themselves, that they <u>are</u> the body. However, the body is made of the Earth elements and is actually the body of the Earth which holds the consciousness of the Earth in the DNA. It is only by placing the body concept in a correct perspective that the Ego can return to expressing Light - from its Light Body.

268

Earth Ascension:

Ascension is the transformation and movement of a conscious being into higher frequencies of Light. The increasing consciousness and Light flowing through more and more Earth-bodies is increasing the Light of the Earth, which is developing a consciousness and Light that will create a direct contact with the energies of the Fourth-dimension. Once this process is completed, the Earth Children - its bodies, will exhibit characteristics which will blend the Light frequencies of both the Third and Fourth dimensions. This will effectively expel all dominance and control of the Illusion and the Astral Lords.

Ego:

The Human Ego is a permanent frequency of One Light. It exists on the lower frequencies of the Fourth-dimension and acts as a lens to focus Light to the Earth and its bodies. It has a dual essence, of an intellectual nature and a feeling nature. The feeling nature is often referred to as the Soul of Man.

Etheric:

Etheric energies are those energies of an electrical frequency similar to the energies of the Sun. These etheric energies are actually responsible for the maintenance of the form of the body. They are Third-dimensional energies and are the highest frequencies of this dimension.

Light Body:

The Light Body is the "higher dimensional self" which is fragmented throughout several dimensions due to the Ego focusing its frequencies mainly in the Illusion. By turning your Ego away from the Illusion, you allow connection of your Light Body with the Earth-body, and can become One Light again.

Solar Gate:

The solar gate is the point where the Fourth and Fifth dimensional frequencies pass through to this Third-dimensional universe. Similar entry points exist through all the stars of this universe.

"The Ionic Body"
by
Dr. Douglas Jesse.

"Why guess when you can be sure?"
Our modern world views health in so many confused ways that it is difficult for the health seeker to know which path to follow.

It is becoming understood that energy medicine holds the key to a more fundamental approach to the healing of the body, yet still the approach is fragmented by the numerous varieties of modalities available.

We all want certainty of success in the treatment of our health problems, and we want to know how to maintain that good balance of health once it it is achieved.

The "Ionic Body" tells you what health is, and how it can be attained and kept. One simple equation is the secret to optimum health.

1.5 6.4 / 6.4 6.6C 0.04M 3 / 3
These are the Magic Numbers of Health!

A simple equation - a simple test of health.
<u>But a dynamic idea!</u>
The "Ionic Body" explores the equation and reveals many interesting facts about your body.

If you wish to know what your body requires for absolutely amazing health, then read this book.

Available from Light Pulsations: In Australia $23.00.
Overseas: $30.00.

- Light Pulsations -

Light Pulsations is an Australian company dedicated to promoting books and products which produce health and expansion of consciousness in all who use them.

Our products include books on health and spiritual awareness; homeopathic health remedies; health analysis kits; and education courses in the field of Natural Healing and Ionictherapy, through The Universite Homeopathique du Pacifique.

Our philosophy is to make this planet a better place in which to live and grow, through the upliftment of the individual, for all change begins at this level.

Write to us for our catalogue of books and products, which will alter your life in a most positive manner.

****

In 1998, *Light Pulsations* will be publishing a boxed set of cards and accompanying book, **"The Oracle to Freedom"** Write to have your name registered for advanced notification when these become available.